The crisis in modern social psychology

Critical Psychology

Series editors

John Broughton
Columbia University

David Ingleby
Vakgroep Ontwikkeling en Socialisatie, Utrecht

Valerie Walkerdine
University of London Institute of Education

Since the 1960s there has been widespread disaffection with traditional approaches in psychology, and talk of a 'crisis' has been endemic. At the same time, psychology has encountered influential contemporary movements such as feminism, neo-marxism, post-structuralism, and post-modernism. In this climate, various forms of 'critical psychology' have developed vigorously.

Unfortunately, such work — drawing as it does on unfamiliar intellectual traditions — is often difficult to assimilate. The aim of the Critical Psychology series is to make this exciting new body of work readily accessible to students and teachers of psychology, as well as presenting the more psychological aspects of this work to a wider social scientific audience. Specially commissioned works from leading critical writers will demonstrate the relevance of their new approaches to a wide range of current social issues.

Titles in the series include

The Crisis in Modern Social Psychology
Ian Parker

The Psychology of the Female Body
Jane M. Ussher

Significant Differences
Corinne Squire

$ 12.95

57609

The crisis in modern social psychology
and how to end it

Ian Parker

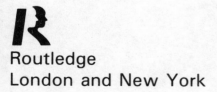

Routledge
London and New York

First published 1989
by Routledge
11 New Fetter Lane, London EC4P 4EE
29 West 35th Street, New York, NY 10001

© 1989 Ian Parker

Typeset by J&L Composition Ltd, Filey, North Yorkshire
Printed and bound in Great Britain by
Biddles Ltd, Guildford and King's Lynn

British Library Cataloguing in Publication Data
Parker, Ian, *1956–*
    The crisis in modern psychology: and how
    to end it.— (Critical psychology)
    1. Social psychology. Methodology
    I. Title   II. Series
    302'.01'8

Library of Congress Cataloging in Publication Data
Parker, Ian, *1956–*
    The crisis in modern social psychology, and how to
    end it.
    (Critical psychology series)
    Bibliography: p.
    Includes index.
    1. Social psychology. I. Title. II. Series.
HM251.P29 1989   302   89–5938
ISBN 0–415–01493–X
      0–415–01494–8 (Pbk)

Contents

Acknowledgements   vii
Introduction   1

Part one: 'Crises'   7

1 The paradigm crisis   11
   Placing paradigms   12
   Experimentation and ethogenics   18
   Problems: ideology and power   23

2 The political crisis   29
   History and power   30
   Psychology and sociology   32
   The individual and the crowd   35
   Social psychology as a discipline   42

3 The conceptual crisis   48
   Structuralism, semiology and hermeneutics   49
   The contexts of post-structuralism   55
   Contradictions   61

Part two: Responses   67

4 Ordinary explanation   72
   Attribution theory   74
   Deconstructing attribution theory   80
   Deconstructing ethogenic responses   84

5 Social representations   90
   'Social representations'   91
   Sociological representations   95

Contents

Social paradigms 98
Representation, structure and struggle 103

6 Conversation 108
Readings 108
Sociality and textuality 111
Speakers and listeners 116
Writers and readers 120

Part three: Alternatives 127

7 Culture 131
Postmodernity and language 131
Post-politics 138

8 Politics 141
Fatal attraction 141
Star wars 144
True stories 147
Back to the future 150

Further reading 158
References 161
Index 169

Acknowledgements

Early versions of chapters in this book have reached a reader-friendly state through the efforts of colleagues and students struggling with wild ideas. Special thanks for support to Bob Anderson, John Broughton, Erica Burman, Alan Costall, Peter Dews, Anthony Easthope, Richard Gidwaney, Roger Ingham, Rom Harré, Martin Hewitt, Jan Hilton, Kath Holland, Reinier Holst, Ann Jones, Jean Ledigo, Patrick O'Grady, Jonathan Potter, John Riach, Russell Spears, Valerie Walkerdine, Heather Walton, and Amanda Woolfson.

Introduction

This book is about one of the smaller, dustier corners of the human sciences. Some readers will, I guess, be trapped there, having painted themselves in. There will be a mixture of personal and career investments and, perhaps, a desire to know what makes people tick in social situations. More to say to them in a moment.

Readers outside the discipline will probably know something of the exciting debates which have occurred in the last two decades over the uses of post-structuralism in the human sciences. They may be aware of the contention of some philosophers and historians that we have entered a new cultural period, postmodernity, in which we experience writ large, in everyday social relations, the processes of language to which post-structuralism attends. Maybe they have turned to this book precisely to look a little more closely at what those social relations, and a study of them, would be like.

Social psychology should be about changes in the real world. It should also, though, be concerned with how people can collectively *change* the order of things for themselves. Unfortunately, social psychology as an academic institution is structured in such a way as to blot out what is most interesting about social interaction (language, power, and history) and to divert attention from efforts to de-construct its oppressive functions in a practical way. This is partly why social psychology deservedly gets such a bad press.

This sorry state of affairs can be turned to advantage, though. I suggest that this book be read in two ways. First of all I will focus on social psychology as an example of how a sub-area of the human sciences seals itself off from the outside world, and how it simultaneously crystallizes as a disciplinary apparatus. Issues to do with the 'ordinary explanations' people give of their actions, the shared social knowledge they employ to account to others, and the rhetoric which guarantees their power, are filtered through, and distorted by, this apparatus. The description I give of the crisis in social psychology and the proposals put forward to end it open out into general issues of ideology, power, and the culture of which it is a part. Social psychology supports modern culture, 'modernity', in which the world is experienced by people as tied together by stories of humanized science, progress, and individual meaning. These stories, or 'metanarratives', have supposedly broken down as a new postmodern culture is arising.

Second, despite the uninteresting (and sometimes ludicrous) way social interaction is re-defined in the discipline, I do not want to imply that social phenomena which lie at the border of our individual activities and of social structures, should be simply explained away. They are not irrelevant, and so each discussion in the following pages of things like ordinary explanation, belief, and conversation links them with their wider-ranging political and cultural effects. If we can rescue our understanding of such social–psychological things from the grip of social psychology we can tackle power and engage politically with our present oppressive cultural arrangements from the base up. This book deconstructs social psychology. I show how attempts to improve it have failed, and why we need instead a political understanding of social interaction which links research with change.

Such suggestions will sound a mite treacherous to readers inside social psychology. Would this not involve putting in jeopardy the whole enterprise of social psychology? Possibly. However, other societies have functioned perfectly well without a discipline of social psychology (or even psychology) and there is no reason to believe that future societies could not also do without it. In fact, if the theories of language and power advanced by post-structuralists and by the diagnosticians of postmodernity are right, we need to be sceptical about the disciplinary practices we reproduce and the self-images we propagate. Positive images should not have the function of humanizing the present, and legitimizing it, but they are spaces for resistance to power and ideology.

The moral of the story presented in the following pages, and of the political analysis offered at the end of the book, could be drawn out in different ways depending on where you stand in relation to social psychology. There will be some readers who will have wandered unwittingly or unwillingly across the borders of our land. They may discover that the state of things here is as bad as they suspected, and decide to keep out. To be honest, there are much richer and more sophisticated discussions of post-structuralism and politics in anthropology, sociology, and history, and more interesting descriptions of subjectivity in literature, philosophy, and cultural studies.

A second group of readers, students who have started to study social psychology, will have made some small commitment to the subject. Perhaps they will have become exasperated at the reductionism in psychology generally, and in what passes as 'social' psychology. They might be encouraged at the prospect of moving beyond fixations on the prediction and control of behaviour and press for their teachers and course texts to address seriously the key issue of how we live our lives and how we could do so otherwise. This group is in the relatively strong position of being able to make demands for relevance and some political sensibility in the study of social interaction. This is not an invitation for a long march through the institutions of social psychology. On the contrary, such demands could be more easily made by those who will always be outside (and whose career investments are not at risk).

The third and final group of readers are those who will be hardest to please and most immune to the arguments in these pages. I have, reluctantly, to count myself in this group. We have absorbed much of the jargon of a discipline that is either irrelevant to people outside academic institutions or is just plain deceitful and unpleasant in the picture it paints of human beings. We are bound into the discipline in two ways: first, through the internalization of the defensive postures we adopt when ridiculed by non-social psychologists at such places as seminars or parties; second, through the pleasure we get from reproducing in our little community the language games which hold it together. A *preliminary* step would be for us to connect what we do and say with changes in culture and abandon the pretence that we can be politically neutral.

The most important part of this book, in fact, is that part which deals with how we may wrench ourselves from the cosy confines of social psychology and link up with debates in other disciplines. This involves being critical about our own history, and asking continually whether, by our activities and theories, we are re-producing or *disrupting* oppressive social practices. As will become clear in the course of the following chapters, the term 'ideology' must mean more than merely a 'set of beliefs' to have any critical purchase on the theories I will be discussing. I will argue that post-structuralism is useful, but that we have to retain the term 'ideology' (despite the protestations of fervent foucauldians or derisive derrideans) for political purposes.

An adequate notion of ideology must include an appreciation of the importance of *conflict*, and so I will argue that we should understand ideology as the effects of power relations in discourses and texts. These power relations are signalled through conflicts over meaning. Similarly, our analysis of 'power' must pose, at the very moment we use the term, a *resistance* to its operations. I understand power to be the reproduction of relations between people in which resistance is suppressed. I hope that the proposals in the final chapter for a programme of research and activity will at least provoke some debate among radical social psychologists, and that something useful will emerge from the debris of the discipline.

There *are* social psychologists, but this does not necessarily mean that it would ever be possible to have a coherent radical social psychology. The way the tensions erupted into the 'crisis' in the discipline some fifteen or so years ago is proof that a radical opposition does exist. The problem is that it is fragmented, and the criticisms and alternatives levelled against the 'old-paradigm' laboratory–experimental approach by partisans in the crisis debates were insufficient. Most of the arguments were simply recuperated (absorbed and neutralized) and are still being recuperated today. That process is analysed in this book.

The precondition for such an analysis, however, is an appraisal of the value of critical arguments during the course of the crisis. At the heart of these conflicts was the self-styled 'new paradigm' *ethogenic* social psychology. A simple definition of ethogeny can also serve as an explanation for the word. Ethogeny is the application of ethological methods (the careful observation of the functions of animal behaviour) to speaking beings, human beings who can give accounts of what they are up to. These accounts, which seem simply to be about what people do, also do things themselves. Spoken (and written) accounts do not only describe, they also change the world, and they change relations between people. Once you grasp that, you are thrown into the midst of debates about the power of language in social life.

Ethogenics marked out a little niche for itself by virtue of its anti-experimental stance, but it also made a bid for the humanist vote by turning to the accounts people offer as an alternative to traditional methodologies. This is one of the reasons why it steered clear of an explicit engagement with post-structuralist ideas. It is necessary to recognize the influence of the ethogenic writings, but also, crucially, we have to insist that the crisis in social psychology is not over. It is, then, with those issues that I will begin.

Part one

'Crises'

Social psychology is in permanent crisis. Or rather, it may be more accurate to say that it is racked by a number of intersecting *crises*. I will show that the continual crises which have upset social psychologists in the last decade and a half are part of the *structure* of the discipline. Moreover, the crises are not a matter internal to, or peculiar to, social psychology.

Social psychologists have suffered the weight of political struggles around their discipline ever since its inception at the beginning of the century. If we want to find our way out of the tangle of contradictions which return time and time again to destroy the value of each 'discovery' we think we have made about social phenomena, we must have some sense of what the struggles *outside* the discipline are. As we will see in this part of the book, social psychology excludes the crucial interconnected issues of ideology, power, and history in two ways; by denying developments in other academic areas, and by repressing its own past.

In these first three chapters I deal in turn with (1) the so-called 'paradigm shift' in the discipline, (2) the political background to the conflicts which structure it, and (3) the conceptual debates which run parallel to it in other human sciences. We will then be better armed to deal, in Part two, with the array of 'responses' offered us in recent years by both the old 'paradigm' tradition and the new loyal opposition. In Part three I will then locate contemporary debates in a cultural context and explore some political options.

Chapter one

The paradigm crisis

What is a paradigm? There are many different contradictory definitions, and even radical social psychologists wanting to appeal to Kuhn's (1970) analysis of the structure of scientific revolutions must realize that he used the term 'paradigm' in at least twenty-one ways. More than that, the paradigms Kuhn described were paradigms in the natural sciences, not the *human* sciences. If a paradigm is a framework of assumptions, then we could see traditional social psychology as being governed until the early 1970s by a paradigm which told us that we should understand individual behaviour by accumulating laboratory-experimental data. 'New' social psychology sold itself as a more advanced paradigm which told us to take accounts seriously. But it is not as simple as that.

Social psychology as a human science does not shift inexorably forward as it assimilates 'facts' and accommodates itself to the 'real' world (however much it may pretend to). One of the images at work in the paradigm story is that of *progress*. The other image which guides us through analyses of the problems of everyday life is that of a *perception* which changes, but is supposedly moving towards a closer and closer correspondence to truth. These two ideas would appear, explicitly or implicitly, in any traditional definition of scientific paradigm change. The problem is that social psychology involves neither progress nor perception.

On the contrary, because social psychology is about a social reality which changes with culture and history, we would be quite wrong to imagine that 'facts' are the spanners in the works which force through 'paradigm shifts'. Critics of traditional laboratory-experimental social psychology a decade and a half ago actually used the terms 'old paradigm', 'new paradigm', and 'paradigm shift' self-consciously as rhetorical constructions (Harré and Secord 1972). 'New' ethogenic social psychologists and their fellow travellers in the discipline do not claim to describe the 'real' state of an enterprise which pretends to be a science: their descriptions are designed to construct, disrupt, and change that state.

Placing paradigms

If we consider the fictions which hold together the paradigms of pretend sciences like social psychology, we find that it is impossible to get very far without discussing their cultural and political contexts. The notion of progress, for example, is appealing, but the problem is that it invites us to sketch a blueprint for a future state by using *present* materials and concepts. This would restrict our options. A bigger problem is that the idea of 'progress' itself is a peculiarly modern one which originated in Anglo-American culture in the eighteenth century and gathered steam in the industrial revolutions of the nineteenth. A belief in 'progress', then, promises to release us from modern times while actually shackling us to them. The notion is culturally specific. There is nothing 'true' about it. If it is put under pressure, then the idea of progress collapses into an opposite: relativism.

Now consider the perceptual metaphor of the *gestalt* switch designed to support and sell the idea of 'paradigms' in science. You are often, in this literature, invited to collude in a little experiment which will confirm a particular model of science and even flatter you into believing that you too are a (naïve) scientist: you see a duck which changes magically into a rabbit and back again. In reality, of course, this model of change is too free-flowing and it needs to be supplemented with an account of the constraints which hold interpretations of a figure as duck or rabbit in place; the 'disciplinary matrix' of the paradigm, perhaps, that Kuhn (1970) describes. Ducks are not rabbits, and it would require a theory of enormous power to persuade us that they were. That power would have to be in some sense coercive. In science the paradigms which inform images of the world, and in social psychology the paradigms which inform our views of people, are coercive. There are, as well as perceptions, *de*ceptions organized into a series of interpretations held in place by language. There are always sets of statements in and around science which tell us how we should see things. Under pressure, the innocent perception collapses into an opposite: text.

One lesson of these brief deconstructions of progress and perception, of the hidden tenets of 'scientific' social psychology, is that we must place any discussions of the paradigm shift in a wider frame. That wider frame involves the meanings given to the geographical separation of research traditions. The cultural context of any crisis of paradigms is organized in social psychology by the distribution of economic power in the world, and for most social psychologists that is mediated by the relationship between America and Europe. The criticisms of positivism and individualism and the flight from the laboratory correspond to an increasing interest in European social psychology. While the struggle of partisans of the European approach against the regime of American social psychology is not confined to geographical boundaries, it is important that we appreciate the significance of these sites of tradition and of resistance. I want to explain why American social psychology is often (wrongly) seen as the only problem, with European social psychology (equally mistakenly) offered as the solution.

America

For an English-speaking audience the development of theoretical and research traditions is deeply influenced by the relationship between America and Europe, with American cultural assumptions forming the terms of debates. America is both the home of social psychology as an institution, and the scene of its earliest discontents. From Triplett's (1898) first social psychology experiment on the effect of others on cyclists (in which, bizarre though it may sound, he timed children turning fishing reels), to operationalized studies on 'social facilitation' (where cockroaches were timed running races), the social world in this culture has been depicted as sometimes an occasion for, but always a potential risk to, the *individual*. Alongside this thorough-going individualism is a mechanistic framing of human action.

Enclosed within this overarching narrative about individual autonomy and the social dangers to it are the little stories etched into the social psychologist's imagination and passed rapidly on to new students. Here are the laboratory vignettes of Asch (1952) on

13

conformity and Milgram (1963) on obedience: others in groups can distort your perceptual judgement, and others in command can destroy your moral judgement. Then there are the redescriptions of the real world designed to read as if laboratory phenomena had taken on a life of their own: social processes like 'groupthink' or 'bystander apathy'.

In some cases this was hardly surprising. In the McCarthyite cultural climate after the Second World War – when radical psychologists could lose their jobs for excluding themselves from the 'liberal' consensus – proposals for a 'new social psychology' looked beyond the 'armchair' and 'data-collecting' phases to the institutionalization of the discipline. Appeals were made to the interests of the US military: 'when West Point and Annapolis begin to see the importance of a scientific approach to problems of social behaviour, the rest of the country cannot be far behind' (Dennis 1948: 12). However, even when there was the promise of a turn away from the concerns of the state to 'real' problems, social psychologists still reinforced the traditional approaches.

The key demands of psychologists faced with growing un-employment were often simply for more jobs and more research on 'social problems'. It was in this context that the Society for the Psychological Study of Social Issues (SPSSI) was founded at the 1936 American Psychological Association (APA) convention. Activists in the SPSSI did attempt to channel energies in a progressive way by, for example, materially supporting the struggle against fascism in Spain. However, such exceptions to the general preoccupation with defending social psychology were rare (Finison 1977).

The terms of the debate as to the future of psychology were set by the traditional conservative leaders of the APA, with E. G. Boring in the 'restrictivist' camp commending the operation of the law of 'survival of the fittest' to the membership, and groups like the Psychologists' League, speaking for the 'expansionists', demanding jobs (Finison 1976). It was only later that worries were voiced that, without a radical overhaul of methods and conceptions of social behaviour, the treating of social problems would always end up treating the oppressed as 'problems'. Issues such as racism, for example, tended to be addressed from the point of view of the oppressors (which in this case had much to do with the exclusion of black people from psychology). In contrast, when the paradigm crisis erupted in the 1960s and 1970s, in the context of radical social movements outside and inside the universities and colleges, radicals were able to breach the boundaries around social psychology, and raise both interdisciplinary and political issues.

While America is the home of social psychology, it is also the home of the crisis in social psychology. This is due to the close connection between the discipline and the concerns of the economy and state, the character of American society as a free-enterprise capitalism carried to a degree way beyond the dreams of European entrepreneurs, and the consequent heightening of tensions between radical European social theory and the mechanistic individualism embodied in the laboratory experiment. Most of the American crisis literature is simply about such things as the frivolity of experiments, the ethics of deception, or the need to learn from subjects. This, at least, is the literature cited now. There were actually many complaints at the end of the 1960s about the alienating character of American society. There was a widespread disenchantment with psychology and the culture that spawned it. However, as will be seen in Chapter two, this cultural explanation does not colour in the whole picture.

Europe

Those who were outside America were able to link the debates inside social psychology with cultural issues more readily. They had, after all, been sold a vision of social relations which was not just wrong or 'alienating'. When European social psychologists got the approach home it did not work. Hence characterizations in the British crisis literature of the 'American paradigm' and, more to the point, in the French literature (relayed to an English-speaking audience through *The European Journal of Social Psychology*) of the impact of ideology on social science and its attempts to eradicate conflict (Moscovici 1972; Plon 1974).

Although the revolt against the cultural dominance of American laboratory-experimental social psychology in Europe was traced by some writers to the impact of Paris May 1968 events, the concern with 'ideology' as an object of study has deeper roots. European social psychology has historically had a closer relationship with research in sociology and anthropology than the American variety. While recently rehabilitated research on systems of

15

meaning and belief and social conceptions of self (Mead 1934) in America were hived off to sociology and philosophy departments, in France studies of 'social representations' – shared meanings and self-concepts – were being carried out in social psychology at the end of the 1950s. (I will return to this strand of research in Chapter five.)

The interest in sociological ideas and the experience of the old paradigm as a culturally oppressive form led even some of the more politically cautious critics in Europe to implicate the structure of American society in the crimes of laboratory experimentation (Armistead 1974). Harré, for example, in his outlines of an ethogenic new paradigm, includes sideswipes at 'North American mores' which treat 'conduct as the behavioural output of trained automata' (1983: 5). Social psychology is part of the *problem* and not part of the solution, and this is how many radicals read the following appeal in an influential European contribution to the crisis literature:

> The central and exclusive object of social psychology should be the study of all that pertains to *ideology* and to *communication* from the point of view of their structure, their genesis and their function. The proper domain of our discipline is the study of cultural processes which are responsible for the organization of knowledge in a society. (Moscovici 1972: 55)

This proposal is a good one, but the call for the study of ideology as such is not sufficient to constitute a radical alternative to the American tradition. 'Ideology' can easily be sanitized and recuperated by social psychology. A crucial additional ingredient is a notion of *conflict*. Such a notion is either simply absent, or deliberately excluded, from the picture in the American tradition. Instead, the attainment of consensus was the goal of much of the criticism of deception in the experiment, and the outcome of this was the fruitless debates on the value of role-playing, where experiments continued to be carried out but were now reinforced by liberal doses of 'communication' and 'trust'. Alongside this went the weak suggestion that we could 'advance the cause of human welfare' simply by demanding more 'relevance' (Ring 1967: 113).

When there is no notion of conflict, there is little political value in descriptions of psychological knowledge. Where conflict was brought to the fore, however, as in the European social-psychological contributions, we were at least offered an exposé of the way

American social psychology constructed a 'false knowledge' of society and labelled resistance to the social order as unnatural (Plon 1974). The advantage of counterposing the European developments to the American tradition is to throw into question the idea that any particular social order should be considered 'natural' in the first place.

Culture

There are a number of tempting ways to understand the impact of American and European culture on the contours of the crisis in social psychology. The first, obvious, response to the distinction between the two cultures would be that we only have to opt for European social psychology and champion it against bad old American social psychology. This would be a mistake. The new European research contains many unhelpful assumptions of its own. This does not, however, mean that we should simply reject both the American and European variants of the discipline. There are spaces for resistance in both American and European work which are useful and progressive. I will argue below that the new paradigm which emerged from the crisis also contains some useful ideas. A third way which would be more in keeping with the deconstructive approach discussed later on in this book would be to emphasize the European contribution and bring it into sharper conflict with the American research. Out of the conflict will emerge something better (and quite different).

Each variant of social psychology not only describes social phenomena but also, as part of a culture, *creates* and re-produces the social phenomena it studies. The social reality which American and European social psychology participates in is, in part, defined by way of its opposition to the other culture. (We will see the political effects of this in the next chapter, and the consequences for other cultures in Chapter eight.) For the moment, we have to be aware of the way language, as the cartilage of culture, produces, through its own distinct metaphors of social mechanisms, ways not only of understanding the world, but also ways of 'understanding' other ways of understanding the world. This work of language in accounting for action, and becoming part of the action itself, brings us to the alternatives to laboratory experimentation advocated by the ethogenic new paradigm.

Experimentation and ethogenics

In 1976 Middlemist *et al.* published the results of an experiment in the *Journal of Personality and Social Psychology* which continued a long-running tradition of research in America, that of 'social facilitation'. Is the presence of others arousing? Too arousing? To their credit Middlemist and his co-workers moved out of the laboratory. The paper is called 'Personal space invasions in the lavatory: suggestive evidence for arousal'. It reported the effects of proximity (independent variable) on males 'coactively engaged in private elimination' (dependent variable). If the presence of another person increased arousal in the lavatory you would expect two things to happen: muscles at the exit from the bladder would tense and so the delay before the onset of urination would be longer, and the delay and the tension would cause the urine stream to be faster and therefore to persist for a shorter time.

In one situation (control condition) the unwitting subject used the only urinal not closed for cleaning; in another (first experimental condition) one of the experimenters stood at the next urinal; and in another (second experimental condition) the experimenter stood one urinal away. In a pilot study one of the researchers hid inside the toilet cubicle next to the urinal with a tape-recorder, but the background noise was too loud to get usable data. So, in the actual study, the person in the cubicle had a little periscope balanced on some books under the door directed upward so that the subject's urinal was visible. They were then able to observe and measure the delay and persistence of urination accurately.

Significance

The results were 'significant', that is, you can take them with a pinch of salt. The *experiment* is significant for a number of reasons. It is an 'ideal type' (a caricature and exemplar) of the research the new paradigm in social psychology is trying to displace. I will draw out five main points which highlight the problem with this type of old paradigm social psychology, and which lead on to the alternative approaches advocated by those in and around the ethogenic new paradigm.

The first point is that the experiment is American, published in an American journal. The issues that cluster around this point are partly to do with the sheer number of journals available to reproduce the discipline in America and exhaust the (few) good ideas that do crop up from time to time with useless empirical studies, and with the pressure on American academics to churn out studies which are designed for curricula vitae more than anything else. Journals do not usually, in addition, publish *non*-significant results, and most journals do not have a blind refereeing procedure to decide which papers should be accepted (though this in itself would not guarantee anonymity or neutral adjudication on the quality of articles). This is not to say that trivial experiments do not appear in European journals, or that there is not a manic drive there to publish, but American social psychology is particularly badly affected.

The second point is that although the research moved out of the laboratory, the study still, to all intents and purposes, was a laboratory-experimental one. An entirely artificial schema was designed by the researcher in which different variables could be predicted and controlled. This schema was then bolted onto the 'real' world so that no unexpected meanings would intrude. An interpretive frame was constructed around an aspect of the 'real' world such that it becomes understood *as if* it were a tightly controlled experimental setting. (This is not merely a result of the physical characteristics of the research space.) The experiment also required deception.

The third point is to do with the methodological approach which gives rise to the pseudo-scientific description of 'private elimination'. A quantitative approach deliberately screens out the meanings of being in a public lavatory and substitutes measurement of the urine stream. It is just such a delusion of understanding human social experience through the accumulation of measurements and divined causal relations that defines *positivism* in social science.

The fourth point concerns the essential *individualism* which pervades social psychology. Leaving aside for the moment the moral evaluation of the social which informs social-psychological theory and research generally, the framework of 'social facilitation' is built on the effects of individual others on one individual's performance (cycling, writing, micturating). This, we are invited to believe, is social behaviour. More sophisticated theoretical frameworks dealing with 'attitudes', 'attributions', or 'stereotypes' still locate the appropriate machinery inside the head of an individual.

19

Fifth, and last, is the question of history and culture. The sometimes hidden, sometimes explicit agenda of laboratory-experimental social psychology is to absorb the positivistically viewed causal laws obtained from the data of an individual's behaviour into a theory about human beings which is universally applicable. In the present case, the 'theory' of 'social facilitation' loses its power when we ask questions about the historical specificity of 'private elimination'. The defensiveness experienced in public lavatories is just one aspect of the transgression of what we now, in modern times, take to be our sacred individual privacy. To be 'coactively engaged in private elimination' is to be participating in a culturally distinct practice with particular meanings. An additional issue here is that although the traditional focus on white psychology undergraduates is not so overt in the study, we are drawn once again into the world of *male* social activity and conned into extrapolating to 'social facilitation' throughout the whole of humankind.

Signification

But did they speak, these subjects? Imagine one of them turning to leave and accidentally stumbling over the books and periscope. He looks to the experimenter at the next urinal who feels compelled to head off a potentially awkward scene. Well, this is exactly what it is, a 'scene' in which two of the actors must engage in a plausible presentation of a 'social-psychologist' persona, and the third must attempt not to appear foolish. Up to now each action contained meanings carefully screened out by the experimenters in their report of the study. They were tacitly aware of this when they blocked off all urinals but two in the first experimental condition in order to exclude possible embarrassing interpretations of the situation on the subject's part when one experimenter stood next to him. Now the experimental frame has been disrupted, the meaning emerges in language as they account for their actions by saying 'this is a social psychology experiment'. How they could account, with shared meanings, is the subject matter of the ethogenic new paradigm social psychology.

Ethogenic alternatives which emerged out of the crisis incorporate a number of ideas from analytic philosophy (Austin 1956) and microsociology (Garfinkel 1967; Goffman 1971; Mead 1934). The broad approach is not simply a theory and method for studying social interaction, for its proposals entail a view of society which has moral and political consequences. A brief summary of the ethogenic approach can be hung on three points: the idea of an expressive order, a description of that order as drama, and an understanding of social rules.

The first point is one which calls upon a crucial and fruitful distinction we should make between the *practical* and the *expressive* orders (Harré 1979). Sleeping, eating, and excreting are activities which must be performed by human beings as biological organisms in order to survive. Such practical matters could be carried out by a Robinson Crusoe, but many others are needed to reproduce wider-reaching material structures: hunting and cooking food, tilling the land, building factories, or information technology hardware, are all part of the practical order. We can broaden this notion of a practical order to include the different physical locations of bodies in different economic systems and the laws of those economies (trade cycles, 'long waves', and the suchlike) which organize, and occasionally disrupt, human life.

Even a basic biological function like going to the loo, however, is organized in the expressive context of a culture. The unwitting subject in the Middlemist *et al.* experiment could have publicly wet his trousers (to protest against the length of a lecture) or peed against a tree (to show off to the lads). In the lavatory he could have chatted amiably to the stranger next to him or huddled silently over the urinal. Such expressive activities warrant and explain practical activities, and, of course, the system of explanations we use in the expressive order then rebounds on the way we materially structure the practical order. Think of the effects of Lysenko's genetics as an account designed to express a view of the world and *impress* those who held power in the bureaucracy on the practice and products of Soviet agriculture. Ethogenics has been concerned with the way that the expressive order dominates and shapes the practical order. We are told that 'only in exceptional circumstances does the practical dominate social life' (Harré 1979: 35). (We will return to consider what 'exceptional circumstances' may be in Chapter eight.)

The second point of the ethogenic position is to do with how people organize themselves in the expressive sphere to impress others. An ethogenic principle is that life should be viewed as a *drama*. The 'social worlds' of seminars, families, or revolutionary cells are occasions for many dramas to be played out, and each script calls for a different appropriate persona. Many social personas cluster around a single biological organism. Two further issues are involved here. On the one hand, individual agency is primarily directed to the attainment of honour and the avoidance of shame. This is important, for hidden in the common-sense view of people that ethogenists appeal to with the slogan 'for scientific purposes treat people as if they were human beings' (Harré and Secord 1972: 84) is a model (actor, accounter, rhetorician) of what human beings are like. We could use this to pick out 'respect/ contempt' hierarchies in each scene. However, this order and meaning is *shared*, and so is potentially transparent to all social actors. The re-presentation and re-interpretation of behaviour is a precarious business, but one in which everyone can engage equally.

The dramatic social worlds of the expressive order, then, are wrought out of the meanings of behaviour. These meanings emerge as behaviour, or movements become understood as actions designed to accomplish certain acts. To crouch with your head bent over a hollow tube inscribing marks on paper is a series of *movements*. To look down a periscope and to record observations is an *action*. To be performing a social psychology experiment is an *act*. In order to glue their actions into a common understanding of the act that the puzzled subject can participate in, the revealed experimenters would have to rule out definitions of the situation which saw the actions contributing to, say, the meaning of the act as a stake-out or as a seduction. An ethogenic researcher would attempt to gather accounts from the participants in such a social world. Such accounts simultaneously warrant and re-create actions and acts.

The third point of the ethogenic approach is that the social worlds are conceived *as if* they were held together by 'rules'. Some social episodes (weddings, examinations, initiation rituals) are explicitly scripted with the rules written down. A person subjected to social skills training, for example, will be instructed how to speak, when, and to whom. In this case the correlates of a system of social rules, the 'roles' of speaker and listener which should be adopted, are clearly defined. Most social episodes, however, are enigmatic, structured by implicit rules which it is the job of the researcher to elicit.

Our poor subject, however, must be initiated from scratch into the social world of the social psychology experiment, and that process of initiation raises many issues about the status of the rules. One suggestion is that the rules are, in some sense, 'real'. Social psychology could in this way become a 'realist' science. Instead of the non-existent causal laws sought by positivist social psychologists, the ethogenist aims to uncover underlying patterns which have 'powers' by virtue of their employment by human agents. The notion of a rule in itself is only a 'metaphorical device' which refers to those underlying patterns. This line of argument is given a different emphasis on different occasions: sometimes the rules are seen as wholly collective, more often they are imagined to be present within individuals as 'cognitive templates' (Harré 1979).

In contrast to this, an ostensibly more radical ethogenic perspective would focus on the new senses of the situation constructed through initiation into it. The subject is not being implanted with templates but interpreting the scene jointly with the experimenters. In this view, the rules would be understood as an artefact built for the convenience of the researcher and the 'reality' of the situation would be more 'mundane' (Shotter 1984). While Harré would attempt to 'explain' social behaviour using a realist approach akin to structuralism, Shotter attempts to 'understand' what is going on by interpreting action in a manner similar to hermeneutics. Structuralism is an approach characterized by the search for underlying rules which organize meaning regardless of the speaker's intention, while hermeneutics aims to discover the personal sense given by individuals. With these differences, of course, we are opening out into some of the contradictions, limitations, and problems of the new paradigm.

Problems: ideology and power

Contradictions riddle the new paradigm, in part, because it is impossible to construct one watertight systematic theory to account for human behaviour and experience. However, the particular limitations and contradictions of the new social psychology also result from its failure to incorporate key issues which were addressed by radical critics inside the discipline at the height of the crisis and before ethogenics became the new loyal opposition. The key issues are ideology and power. Problems of culture, which are discussed by new social psychology, can be re-cast and re-solved

23

only when the work of ideology and power in social relations is understood.

Language and ideology

The role of language in shaping thought is, of course, often stressed in social science, but it has been given a new lease of life by the descriptions of 'paradigm shifts' Kuhn (1970) offers in science. However, the radical dynamic of this work goes far beyond liberal psychological assertions that we each do, or could, see things differently. Scientific debates and differences do not hinge on perceptions of ducks and rabbits, but on bigger, politically-charged questions about the nature of the world and of human relationships – and paradigm changes here are a good deal nastier, messier, and more machiavellian.

In a discipline which studies human relationships it is impossible to evade those issues. Even so, the crucial move to a conception of ideology and the reproduction of illusion has been firmly blocked in both old *and* new social psychology. Influential ways of blocking a serious study of the role of ideology have included treating it as if it were simply a 'belief system', and pretending that ideology is no longer relevant in a 'post-industrial' society. Both of these (deeply ideological) positions are rooted in American social science, but, as we shall see in future chapters, they have powerful echoes in European theory.

If we take up one of the European social psychological proposals – to turn social psychology to study 'everything that pertains to *ideology* and to *communication*' (Moscovici 1972: 55) – we should take care that we do not simply treat language, ideology, and communication as if they were the same thing. For example, one way of describing the discourse of experimental psychology is to treat it as a set of statements about imaginary cognitive para-phernalia which is parasitic on everyday language. We need to go further than this, however, if we want to follow the radical crisis literature and show how this set of statements presents itself as eternal truth, which 'dehumanizes' its subjects, and 'depoliticizes' social science. Then we must include in our description of ideology what the set of statements *does* and what institutional functions the statements serve. Here, the notion of 'discourse' as a system of statements is particularly useful. Such systems of statements construct 'objects' (like 'stereotypes' or 'attributions'). They call these objects into being, and people then talk about them as if they really did exist. This is how psychological and social-psychological phenomena are created as individual 'things' (Parker 1987a). These matters would have to be integrated into an adequate account of ideology. (You will be in a better position to understand ideology as the combined effects of power relations in discourses and texts when I have considered developments in post-structuralism outside social psychology in Chapter three.)

The overall project of the new paradigm has been to rescue and rehumanize the poor subjects and their essentially good 'common sense' or their 'ordinary language'. The few comments on ideology to be found in ethogenic literature logically extend this preoccupation with the supposed harmony of shared social meaning and have been concerned with redescribing 'false consciousness' as a person's lack of the full accounting repertoire of the expressive order in a community (Harré 1977). A related point here is the way new social psychology conceives of the 'rules' which hold a social world together. Although these rules are not universal, as an ethologist would suspect, they are all too often unquestioned. Ethogenists such as Harré (1980) and Shotter (1975) often place themselves in the 'ordinary language' tradition of British analytical philosophy and implicitly endorse the conservative view propounded in British analytical philosophy, that 'our common stock of words embodies all the distinctions men have found worth drawing, and the connections they have found worth marking'(Austin 1956: 46).

It may well be that the 'common stock of words' gives *that* author all the distinctions he finds worth drawing, but this could be something to do with the fact that he is, among other things, a man. Women would probably want to draw other distinctions which identify the sexist organization of the English language and the way speakers who refer to 'men' conceptually screen out the existence of women. The ideological aspect of ethogeny flows from its inability to take seriously the *conflicts* within the shared community of social meanings that they look to, and sympathetically research, in alternatives to the asocial meaningless laboratory experiment. In contrast, a theme of this book is that at every point where ideology is discussed, the notion of conflict must be ready to hand. At best, the ethogenic new paradigm ignores the sexist, racist, and class-based character of 'ordinary language'. At worst, it produces those oppressive social relations in a theory of consensual meaning. In addition, there is hardly ever an acknow-ledgement of the debt the 'new' methodology owes to feminist work in social science (Stanley and Wise 1983). If, on the other hand, we want to move beyond this to understand how ideology binds a community together in a coercive way, we also need an account of power.

'Powers' and power

Just as the system of ideas in a scientific paradigm binds a community together expressively, so a system of social relation-ships in an institution binds people together *practically*. One of the significant points about social psychology is that, unlike the natural sciences it mistakenly believes it models itself on, it enmeshes those who are outside the 'scientific' community in its operations. Not only are social psychologists bound into the system of social relationships which make up the discipline, but the discipline also reaches out and, through the laboratory experiment, subjects others.

Many of the early criticisms of the laboratory-experiment method – on problems of 'demand characteristics' and 'experimenter effects' – also cry out for some account of the power of the experimenter as 'scientist'. The Milgram electric shock study of obedience, for example, which was able to recast the 'dispositional cement that binds men [sic] to systems of authority' (Milgram 1963: 371) inside the laboratory was a clear demonstration of American scientists' ability to manipulate and coerce an unwitting public. If such authoritarian power relations are so ubiquitous in old social-psychological research, why have they not become a topic of inquiry in new social psychology? In part, this absence is a result of the conception of power which has endured throughout the crisis, and which continues into ethogenic views of the person.

The traditional model of power in social psychology is concerned with the activities of a 'power-holder', and the way in which this person can draw on resources to give reward, punishment, and so on to exercise power over the 'power-subject'. Experimental studies sometimes take into account the power-subject's perceptions and wants, but the overall guiding definition of power is still that it is held and wielded to produce 'intended effects' (Schopler 1965).

This is, of course, an individualistic model of power. It always traces power to a single person. Similarly, when ethogenics talks of the human agent, it is concerned with the 'powers' of individuals and the way those 'powers' may be recognized and investigated. Here more is at stake than a moral claim, for ethogenics demands some account of underlying structures and gives descriptions of the activities of beings attributed with sovereign 'powers'.

This individualist view of power is reinforced by the dramaturgical metaphor which new social psychology uses to understand social life. While one tactic of traditional social psychology was to study individuals who were particularly 'machiavellian', new social psychology took the position that we are all negotiating our way through the impression–management games and 'moral careers' which make up the social order. Some microsociological descriptions had signalled a debt to Machiavelli and emphasized the importance of power, but new social psychology has stressed instead the positive natural desire for 'respect' within the expressive sphere which drives the person to get one up on others. Once this position is adopted, there are risks that the desire to take *all* accounts in good faith would have dangerous political consequences (Billig 1977).

Unfortunately, the assertion that the expressive sphere dominates the practical order eventually leads new social psychology to bizarre claims that there is, really, no such thing as power at all; it can be glossed as a mere 'accounting resource' (Harré 1979: 233). Not only do these claims exclude power from the picture (except as an 'accounting device'), but the accounts of *resistance* also disappear from the new social psychological research. Were we to re-introduce such accounts we would also be led to analyse the ideological processes which inhibit or empower them. If we want to develop an adequate understanding of power we have to link any definition of it to a notion of resistance. Power reproduces particular relations between people in such a way that resistance is suppressed. The supporting argument for this definition also requires an account of historical and cultural contexts of action.

Culture and history

When paradigms change it is often the case that views of the 'self' also change. Experiences of the relations between the self and the world and between the self and others alter dramatically. The discovery that the Earth moved round the Sun, for example, displaced the human being from the 'centre' of the universe. Changes in cultural organization involve transformations in subjectivity. We have to attend to the transformations and the differences in subjectivity at different times and in different places, and not to simply slip into a sentimental (and ethnocentric) humanist position. One of the advantages of an ethogenic 'anthropological' perspective on modern life is that it does take other anthropological work on the self seriously (Heelas and Lock 1981), and recognizes that social psychological phenomena are historically transient (Gergen 1973). The problem is that without an understanding of ideology and power this does not go far enough. It can also easily fold back into humanist variants of traditional American psychology.

One of the characteristics of American psychology has been the influence of the humanist opposition to mechanistic, 'dehumanizing', experimentation. As we will see in future chapters, this 'alternative' *complements* what it is against. A humanist position blocks an understanding of ideology and power. A study of ideology and power in social psychology would also have to turn around to examine the place of 'new' variants of these phenomena. These are issues which require some appraisal of how the practical interacts with the expressive sphere, how conceptions of 'honour' change, and how we might mark our own critical distance from what new social psychology describes. What is the relationship between ideological conflict and resistance to power in the transformation of one research paradigm to another, and what are the social conditions which support and enjoy such debates? There are exceptional circumstances in which the expressive sphere is disrupted by the practical order of society, and many of these have affected social psychology. A first step to an investigation of the relationship between culture and subjectivity in the discipline must be a critical history of the conditions of its birth.

Chapter two

The political crisis

The crisis in social psychology reflects economic and political crises in the culture in which it arose. Power accompanied the development of the discipline, and resistance to those power relations was defeated so that the future of social psychology was assured. These power relations must be uncovered and understood before they can be undone. To do this entails writing an unashamedly partisan 'history', and contesting the positions which laboratory-experimental social psychologists thought they had won. As I reinterpret those past events we will move beyond traditional conceptions of power, and will see that we also need to move beyond a mere history of an academic subject to develop a history of the *human* 'subject' – the peculiar malleable and asocial being – who appears time and time again in the research literature. I will return to this subject towards the end of the chapter.

We are told that social psychology took off as a science with the first experiment on 'social facilitation' (Triplett 1898) before the beginning of the century, and that previous theories of social behaviour in philosophy and sociology merely set the stage for this historic advance: had the laboratory arrived earlier, many of the mistakes and blind alleys in the prehistory of social psychology could have been avoided. Since the discovery of the laboratory the discipline has been portrayed as following the natural trajectory which the first results produced (Allport 1968). Traditional histories of social psychology are written within the parameters of the two main narratives which describe the supposed development of paradigms in science. Social psychology, we are told, moves towards the truth (there is more accurate perception) and demystifies social life as it gets better and better (there is progress).

It would be easy for radical social psychologists to tack on the new-paradigm 'revolution' at the end of the story, and argue that now the potential benefits to humanity can be realized, but outside the laboratory. We should resist this temptation. If we look a little more closely at the foundation of social psychology as an institution, we see a discipline built out of *repression*, a repression which left its marks in latent crises and in structural defences against the possibility of those crises becoming manifest.

History and power

The steps to a history which does not develop a mythology which merely praises successes (and which effectively ratifies the present view of things) would have to include some account of how the official myths came about, how the official 'histories' came to be written and with what effects. Such an account should focus on the operation of power and take as its guiding principle the view that science attains a superior status as a result of political and institutional pressures. At this stage, and for these purposes, I will stick with a fairly conventional view of power. I will move on to a more adequate understanding of how power operates as the story unfolds.

Application

The psychological version of social psychology deliberately de-marcated itself against the sociological versions, and was nurtured from the start by a parent discipline which was riven with conflict. In the 1920s in America psychologists were faced with a crisis of perspectives: what kind of discipline should psychology be, and where should it be going? Alongside these debates an influential 'history' was written which finally settled the disputes and interpreted psychology as an experimental science. This account, manifesto, and programme was E. G. Boring's *A History of Experimental Psychology* (1929). This is not to say that Boring's victory silenced the alternative voices. Instead, it recast the vanquished 'applied' psychology into a real-world helpmate of 'experimental' psychology.

On the losing side of the struggle were those psychologists, and social psychologists, who wanted to take advantage of the revolution in applied research. A *Journal of Applied Psychology* had started appearing in 1917, and figures recovered by Terman from the misleading 'official' statistics presented by the American Psychological Association (APA) showed that by 1921 just over half of the membership was engaged in applied work. Applied psychology, it was said, was 'the pay vein that supports the mine', and some supporters optimistically renamed it 'psychotechnology'. The reduced dependence of psychology on the laboratories made life difficult for dyed-in-the-wool experimentalists: by 1927, for example, the laboratory budget at Harvard was only $148, of which Boring supplied $31 from his own pocket (O'Donnell 1979).

Experimentation

The minority experimentalists, however, were in control of the APA apparatus. Supporters of Boring's position kept the secretariat – the communications centre of the organization – in their grip by manoeuvring and preferment from 1917 to 1928. In addition, there was another group of experimental psychologists outside the APA, led by Titchener, which also influenced the balance of forces inside. At one point Boring's lobbying opened up the opportunity for Titchener to be brought in as President of the APA, a bid which only failed when it became clear that he would only assume office if the vote was unanimous. The difficult atmosphere at conventions and at international meetings organized by the APA personalized these disputes.

The open struggles for power which informed the administrative arrangements in the APA both affected and reflected personal power relations between Boring and his mentor, Titchener. Boring was later to refer to the influence of his 'master' and the way he accepted the insults and arbitrary control Titchener tried to exert over him (Boring 1968). Boring viewed the birth of his own son on Titchener's birthday as a 'tribute', and when Titchener died he felt 'released'. Later attempts by Boring to formulate Titchener's theoretical position were immediately followed by an intense period of psychoanalysis during which the transference recast the analyst as a 'Titchener-substitute'. These power relations with Titchener were then relayed down to others as Boring tried to name an heir in whose future he could make 'the largest investment of identification' (Boring 1968: 50).

In this account I am linking the 'investments' and 'identifications' which drove the individual participants with the academic debates in which they participated precisely because the personal and political aspects of the struggles were so closely welded together at the time. To try to untangle them would simply be to fictionalize a 'neutral' history. Other historians have pointed to the way Boring himself not only organized historical material to suit Titchener, positivism, and the experimentalists, but also hung the material around 'personalities' to fit up the opposition (Danziger 1979). It was during this period that Boring completed *A History of Experimental Psychology* which was a strategic intervention in the 'experimental' vs. 'applied' debate. The book swung things for the experimentalists because it constructed a history which culminated in the ideal of experimentation (O'Donnell 1979).

Psychology and sociology

While these internal debates were raging, psychology was also marking itself off against the discipline of sociology, and this tightening of the disciplinary boundaries was to have a profound effect on the character of social psychology. The creation of boundaries also specified what it would be legitimate to call 'social psychology', and it is necessary now to extend traditional conceptions of power to encompass the force of definitions and interpretations of activity in an accepted 'paradigm'. The traditional view of power which focuses on the activities of a 'power-holder' and on the intentional exercise of power only *partially* accounts for what has been going on so far in the events I have described. This traditional view rests on *psychological* assumptions and emphasizes the control an individual could have over their actions. We now have to move on to a view of power which takes notice of the function and experience of the 'power-subject' (who suffers power) and recognizes unintentional facets of the phenomenon. Power reproduces certain relations between those dubbed 'power-holders' and 'power-subjects', and it suppresses attempts to refuse dominant definitions of the situations in which it operates.

This extended view of power takes on board sociological conceptions of the way the organization of the world also organizes persons. For example, Boring's fealty to Titchener cannot simply be traced to Titchener's exercise of power as 'power-holder'. Boring's recollections of his experience of that power as

'power-subject' involves feelings of being monitored and a com-
pulsion to confess. This should be borne in mind as we trade the
effects of the overall relationship between academic disciplines on
local debates and their participants. It would be too loose to say
simply that psychology (and social psychology) excluded sociology
as the study of society. We have to specify what that 'sociology'
was; in what way it reflects the society it purported to investigate;
what methods it employed; and what the institutional relationship
was between studies of the 'social' and those of the 'individual'.

Sociology and society

Two academic and cultural themes informed studies of social
behaviour before, and then outside, social psychology; social
Darwinism which filtered into psychology, and pragmatism which
has only latterly percolated through the new paradigm breaches in
the discipline. As far as social Darwinism was concerned, Herbert
Spencer and his followers were able to translate the spiritual
precepts of Protestantism into 'natural facts', and prominent
sociologists took up the cause of natural selection in opposing aid
to the poor, state-funded schools, and public health laws. The
combination of divine and natural selection also found disciples in
industry; business was seen as a social complement to the laws of
nature. Once natural selection in the human world could be
identified it could be assisted, by psychologists.

At the same time, the dominant philosophy of educated America
at the time, or at least of the small entrepreneurs, was pragmatism.
For the three key pragmatists, Dewey, James, and Mead, knowledge was an instrument for action. Abstract theoretical work was
secondary to what really worked in the 'real world'. A current of
improvisation in business, and a general dislike of the 'written',
fed into both politics in the form of the New Deal and psychology
in the form of 'applied' work. This meant the rejection of
sociology, and the particular exclusion of the 'philosophical' and
'sociological' pragmatists such as Dewey and Mead. This was
despite their contribution at the turn of the century to psychology
journals (on topics ranging from discussions by Dewey on the
nature of the 'reflex arc' to Mead's references to an 'empirical
community mind'), and it meant that psychology also excluded
itself in a peculiar way from its own culture.

Faith in 'facts'

While pragmatism fed the illusion that anything was possible, an illusion that culminated in microsociology in work on the 'social construction of reality' (Berger and Luckmann 1971), positivism inside psychology was more concerned with knowing what already *was*. Positivism was adopted as the method of the new science, the method supposedly employed by Wundt at the birth of psychology in Leipzig in 1879 and faithfully transmitted by Titchener to America. Social psychology also bought this story and, in its official histories, has roped in Comte from sociology to give a broader 'social' gloss to the method. This conveniently ignores the way that Comte's 'positivism', which was to influence such figures as Durkheim in French sociology, had a philosophical and religious character which is more concerned with the nature of society and ways of reforming it than with the accumulation of separate observations in laboratories. More important still, in this catalogue of distortion, were the interpretations of Wundt's own 'positivist' research.

Wundt was not merely a laboratory-experimental psychologist. His work also influenced sociological work, both by way of his writings and through direct contact with figures such as Durkheim and Mead (Farr 1980). The second half of his career was devoted to a social *Völkerpsychologie* that dealt with the higher cognitive functions which he thought to exist in the group mind (the *Völkseele*). Wundt's 'folk psychology' was not original in Germany, but it required a sociological (Comtean) methodology which was carefully passed over by Americans anxious to translate his earlier experimental work on 'physiological' psychology into a manifesto for individual behaviour (Danziger 1979). Psychology, and then social psychology, was thus able to remain faithful to the more rigorously individualistic cause–effect positivism which it thought reigned in the natural sciences. When Titchener wrote Wundt's obituary in 1921, the later social psychology was depicted as though it were always a 'troublesome subject' for Wundt: it 'furnished a grateful occupation for his old age' (Titchener 1921: 175). The story Titchener told was that Wundt was always really an experimental psychologist but that he fell into social psychology as he stumbled into senility.

Institutional divisions

In social psychology itself hostility to sociology was strengthened
by the competition for attention and resources between psychological social psychology and sociological social psychology (which
I refer to in this book as 'microsociology'). In 1908 an introductory
book – E. A. Ross's *Social Psychology* – addressed a sociological audience, and in the same year William McDougall's *An
Introduction to Social Psychology* was produced for psychologists.
Despite the massive overlap in the content of the two books, Ross's
text was ignored. By the time one of McDougall's students produced his own 'introduction', Ross had been written out of the discipline. Reviews of this book in 1936 were then a pretext for complaints by sociologists that psychologists had unfairly taken 'administrative control' in many universities, and that psychologists had
an inadequate knowledge of social psychology (Bernard 1936).

The institutional estrangement of psychological social psychologists from their erstwhile colleagues in sociology was also
reflected in the membership of academic organizations for the
two groups, the APA and the ASA (American Sociological
Association). By 1937 this contact was minimal. A survey then
found that 22 per cent of the members and associates of the APA
and 24.6 per cent of the ASA declared a specific interest in social
psychology. In all, this amounted to 729 people doing research in
the area. Of this 729, however, only nineteen people held dual
membership of the APA and ASA (Britt 1937). Such administrative exclusion both reflects and reproduces the view that social
psychologists trapped on the psychological side of the institutional
boundary have of other disciplines.

The individual and the crowd

Just as caricatures of sociology led psychology to react by adopting
an extreme *anti*-social research programme, so a caricature of
what social action was led psychology to develop an idealized
model of the 'autonomous' individual. The dreadful images of
what social action could look like when stretched to its worst
degree in collective action were present at the turn of the century
in crowds.

Le Bon's *The Crowd: A Study of the Popular Mind* was
acknowledged by Allport (1968), in the official history of the

discipline, as one of the most influential books in social psychology. The political stance of the book was fuelled by Le Bon's own experience of the 'mobs' in the 1872 Paris Commune and reinforced by the various European fascists who used it as a practical handbook. More important, though, were the descriptions of individuals under the sway of a group mind, and the way those descriptions were linked with popular 'scientific' evolutionary theories. Le Bon drew on contemporary physiological 'discoveries' to explain how the crowd member is reduced, like a hypnotized subject, to the activities of the spinal cord. This state is simultaneously an evolutionary regression to the activities of 'beings belonging to inferior forms of evolution . . . women, savages, and children, for instance' (Le Bon 1896: 36). Out of this theory of the 'group mind' flowed McDougall's description of its nature as a plurality of instincts.

Against this, the experimental social psychologist, F. Allport, argued that the 'group fallacy' was the 'greatest incubus' of social psychology, and that behaviour could be better accounted for when systematically reduced to an individual level: 'if we take care of the individuals, the groups will take care of themselves' (Allport 1919: 229). McDougall's position was specifically rejected by others. This looks like a simple theoretical disagreement: it was not. The concern that mainstream social psychologists wanted to show for individuals extended far beyond doing good positivist science: they wanted to *defend* the individual against the very group processes that they supposed did not exist. We have a striking illustration of the way a discourse – in this case, that of 'the crowd'– can effectively be reproduced by its opponents as well as by willing adherents.

Allport (1927) insisted that the social order brought about a mere 'modification' of an 'original nature'. Nevertheless, at the same time as he was inveighing against the crowd theorists, and widening his criticisms to include those in other disciplines ranging from anthropology to politics, he was busily conducting social facilitation experiments. His doctoral dissertation, for example, was entitled *The Social Influence: An Experimental Study of the Effect of the Group upon Individual and Mental Processes*. The prospect of crowd phenomena seizing individual minds haunted American social psychologists. This theme *organized* social psychology in its infancy. Contemporary reviews of the discipline commented, quite mistakenly, on the disarray in the discipline, and did so because they could not see that the horror of the crowd was everywhere – like the largest letters on a map which are often unnoticed because they fill the most space. One *Outline of Social Psychology* published in 1929 hardly mentions 'the crowd' but the key issues are listed as 'the study of social forces', 'the study of ethnic phenomena', 'the study of collectivist mentality', 'the study of behaviour in groups', and 'the study of mob or crowd phenomena' (Smoke 1935).

Opposition to the crowd and attempts to safeguard individual autonomy were held together by the method of laboratory exper-imentation. Such a method produced its own mechanistic caricature of the rational individual, and should be understood in the context of other discourses powerful at the time. These other discourses were also expressive accounts of rapid changes in the *practical* order. Changes in population, and in the organization of production (practical matters), produced themes of control (expressive de-velopments with practical effects). These changes were catalyzed and compressed by the First World War, an event with practical and expressive repercussions for the organization of the disciplines *and* the study of individual 'subjects'. It is to these changes that I will now turn.

Population

The turn of the century in America saw both an increase in the native (settler) population and an influx of immigrants from Eastern and Southern Europe. This increase was seen as a problem for social reformers and social scientists, and support for Spencer's social Darwinism and for eugenics in both groups, along with simple xenophobia, gave psychologists (many of whom were members of eugenics societies) a peculiarly reactionary voice in local government. Some liberal psychologists, such as Terman, who wanted to generate an 'applied' psychology, were engaged in a 'positive eugenics' through monitoring and developing the strengths of the naturally gifted. Other adherents of eugenics, such as Spearman, were even socialists, but the overall balance was shifting rapidly and inexorably to themes of race improvement.

Those pursuing the struggle against 'feeble-mindedness' carried out the more unpleasant 'negative eugenics' plan for the eradication of the unfit: between 1907 and 1928, over twenty American states had sterilized 8,500 people with the direct connivance of psychologists (Kamin 1974). Slavs and Southern Europeans were particularly victimized, and psychologists were party to the construction of the 1924 Immigration Act (which was later to bar the entry of many European Jewish refugees). In social psychology, McDougall had lamented that practical difficulties militated against the 'elimination' of the 'unfit', but was still to argue, in his *An Introduction to Social Psychology*, that eugenics was part of progressive evolution which would ensure that the fit were selected and the less fit would suffer 'extermination' (McDougall 1908: 254). Population, then, was viewed negatively. Just as contact with masses in crowds could ruin the individual, so an increase in the masses could ruin the nation. The population 'problem' was viewed by social psychologists through the optic of production.

Production

The growing population was absorbed fairly rapidly into an expanding industry. At the turn of the century there was a massive concentration of production: in 1897 the total capitalization of corporations valued at a million dollars or more was $170 million, a figure which rose by 1900 to $5 billion and four years later to $20 billion (Karier 1977). As in all other industrializing nations, however, management experienced the new non-proletarian population as a problem: the workers from rural European (and American) backgrounds were not yet acquainted with the discipline necessary to factory work. Their experience of this discipline and of the power of the employers was developed through resistance, and the crushing of that resistance, during the years in which social psychology was born. In the early years of the century the industrial unions grew in strength and violent mass strikes radicalized them, leading to anarcho-syndicalist splits and clashes with conservative labour leaders in the craft unions. It is important to acknowledge the extent of the resistance to the spread of the new work discipline so that the effects of the defeats under the mechanisms of disciplinary power can be fully appreciated.

Eventually, with little protest from the traditional American Federation of Labor, the state authorities and militias composed of ex-servicemen were brought in to break strikes and destroy the most radical unions. The fate of one of the last major industrial conflicts is especially significant, for the population 'problem' once again reared its head. In 1919 the workers in the Pennsylvania steel valleys struck in protest at low levels of pay (pay which was for a twelve-hour-day seven-day-week). Slav and Italian immigrant workers held out for three months against the House of Morgan – at that time the most powerful monopoly in the world. They were finally defeated by the betrayals of the craft unions and a growing xenophobic hysteria which included the rise of the Ku Klux Klan in the mid-western industrial states. As the obstacles to efficiency in production were systematically eradicated, a system of control was constructed to 'solve' the population problem. It was the success of this system of control which increased production by half between 1918 and 1928 while the factory population actually declined (Davis 1980).

Control

Discourses on the detection of 'feeble-mindedness' and the pernicious effects of crowds on people's minds intersected with social psychology's positivist understanding of the individual at the point of *method*. What was needed was a systematic study of behaviour organized by the ideal of 'prediction and control'. For all the heat of the debates between the applied psychologists and the experimentalists, it is clear now that 'applied' psychology did not so much lose as absorb experimental method and use it in the field, or rather the factory. Developments in industry also spilled back into the laboratory to reinforce social psychologists' adherence to the experiment. The most important of these developments was that of the discourse and practice of Taylorism.

Taylor's *Scientific Management*, first published in 1911, sparked off a craze for efficiency and the systematization of labour control among professional middle-rank engineers. Taylorism bonded together a rapidly expanding sector of industry (with the number of engineers rising from 7,000 to 136,000 between 1880 and 1920), and from this milieu developed a layer of social psychologists keen to take up the call for the building up of a 'science' consisting of 'rules, laws, and formulae' which would 'replace the judgement of the individual workman' (Taylor 1911: 37). Taylor asserted that 'in the past the man has been first; in the future the system must be first' (Taylor 1911: 7), and the organization and calculation of the systems' components was carried out by social psychologists pursuing the aim of 'human engineering'. One manifesto for human engineering extended the scope of this examination beyond work to such things as knowledge of work, the attitude of the employee, loyalty, courtesy, sobriety, housing, and training. Contained in this programme is a conception of normal 'work' against which *abnormal* behaviour could be defined. The system requires unconditional obedience.

By 1918 Taylorism was having a significant influence outside America, and was even, for example, taken up by professional middle managers in the new Soviet state – a fact which augured badly for those fearing the crystallization of a bureaucracy anxious to demand obedience and the restoration of traditional power relations after the destruction of a capitalist economy. Lenin's characterization of scientific management is quite accurate:

> the Taylor system, the last word of progress, is a combination of the refined brutality of bourgeois exploitation and a number of the greatest scientific achievements in the field of analysing mechanical motions during work – the elimination of superfluous and awkward motions, the elaboration of correct methods of work, the introduction of the best system of accounting and control. (Cited in Smith 1983: 13)

Scientific management demanded that the gaze of company management and of social psychologists should penetrate each and every one of the worker's actions. Here was a model framework for conceptually and practically breaking down the mass, whether in the form of crowds or labour unrest, into manipulable individual components. In this way the laboratory became a simulacrum of the workshop and aided the task of positivistically calculating human material. Social psychologists seized on the opportunity to study the effects of different types of factory organization in which the tasks and performance of individual subjects could, according to Allport (1919), be 'instructively varied'. Allport's search for a means of 'acquiring a knowledge of social phenomena sufficiently exact for purposes of prediction and control' (Allport 1927: 383) paralleled, and interacted with, the selection and training of suitable workers from the increasing reserve army of labour.

This is why the 'social facilitation' research took the turn it did when the Triplett (1898) study of children turning fishing reels was written into the literature as the first social psychology experiment. Social psychologists focused on competition. In line with the requirements of 'applied' research, the desire to win was related to the work setting: the aim now – in 1924 – was to examine the influence of rivalry on subjects' performance in simple tasks resembling factory operations. Six years later the next step was to continue the study of 'group effects' but to break them down into yet smaller components; examining, in turn, the effect of 'spectators', 'rivals', 'co-workers', and competing 'overt vocal attitudes' (Dashiell 1930).

This was how the historically constructed problem of population, epitomized for social psychologists in the figure of the crowd, found its solution in production and its 'scientific management'. The scene was now set for the compression of social psychology into a machine for social regulation, a compression accomplished in conditions of internal and international conflict.

War

The First World War fuelled the xenophobia and militarism which divided resistance to Taylorism in industry. The government of President Wilson broke its pledge to keep out of the war, and quickly channelled the attacks on external, European, enemies on to internal, union, enemies. The Russian revolution developed, in part, out of the struggle against that same war. This revolution inspired the American labour leaders to continue the strikes against the Taylor system (which had already led to a commission of inquiry in 1911), but then demoralized and disarmed the struggle when Lenin argued vigorously for the adoption of scientific management. The war also reinforced the American images of European crowds and the hostility to any theoretical framework which might endorse crowd or collective mentality. For the American social psychologist the organic metaphor applied to society (employed by European sociologists such as Durkheim) was an unpleasant and offensive one, as was Wundt's notion of the *Völkseele*. References to the social 'body' were made as warnings, and used by psychologists to draw lessons from the experience of war: the dangers arose when the individual was subordinated 'like a cell in a larger organic unity. Here suggestion may easily become contagion' (Hall 1919: 44).

Wundt, of course, was on the enemy side in the war, though the full extent of his militarism, which he shared with many German psychologists active in both World Wars, was carefully glossed over; Boring ignored it, and Titchener, in his obituary of Wundt, only alluded to it. Other social psychologists were more inclined to exploit the situation. As McDougall (no liberal himself) remarked, 'one good result of the Great War is that we have broken away from the thraldom to theories of German professors to which the scientific world submitted before the war' (cited in Billig 1982: 82). Out of the war, then, sprung a discipline able to profit from the broken labour resistance and manically optimistic about the scientific research which could be carried out on the 'subjects' moulded by the social and political changes. G. Stanley Hall proclaimed,

As we have put more psychology into this war than any other nation, and as we have more laboratories and more men than all others we should henceforth lead the world in Psychology ... Hence the future of the world depends in a peculiar sense upon American psychologists. (Hall 1919: 49)

Social psychology as a discipline

A discipline which was devoted to the study of social behaviour but which was organized, amongst other things, to prevent the 'contagion' of social behaviour spreading, entailed some conception of what would count as 'normal' and 'abnormal'. The rhetoric of the laboratory-experimental social psychology which, according to Allport (1968), saw a great 'flourish' after the First World War, policed the boundary between normality and abnormality in two ways. The first concerned the nature of the individual 'subject' who was the object of research and model of theories in the discipline. The second act of policing concerned the nature of the academic subject and the defences erected against other accounts of social life. The two fit together, of course, and both operate to deny difference, yet at different points in the history of social psychology each has had a particular weight and function.

Normalization

Social psychologists saw a close connection between the study of social behaviour and the identification of deviance. In both areas it was assumed that the deviant processes were not socially organized (through such phenomena as labelling described later in micro-sociology) but must be found *inside* the individual. The guiding theme which flowed into social psychology as it was first formed was that pathologies of individual and social action should be the prime focus of any science of behaviour. In 1921, social psychology found official recognition and house-room when it was incorporated into the title of the *Journal of Abnormal Psychology*. The editors of the journal noted that social psychology probably could not have reached its current status if it had not been for the develop-ments in the 'sister science' of abnormal psychology. If this was true, then it was reasonable to suggest that social psychology could benefit 'in a peculiar way' by discoveries in psychopathology (*JASP* 1921: 2).

This common front against abnormality then set the agenda for the debates between the 'expansionists' in the APA who cam-paigned for more jobs and the 'restrictivists' who saw unemploy-ment as a golden opportunity to prune dead wood throughout psychology. Some 'restrictivist' arguments included appeals for the integration into psychology of the hard natural sciences. This, it was hoped, would not only firm up psychology but also weed out dubious ideas which were a liability to both experimental and applied work. Courses in physics and chemistry, for example, would, in one hard-liner's words, 'serve as a filter to *strain out weak brothers and sisters* who would prefer to study English and Sociology and then turn to Psychology' (emphasis in original, cited in Finison 1977: 749). This proposal quite explicitly links the fortunes of psychology to the exclusion of other disciplines.

Segregation

The hostility to other disciplines drew upon, and reproduced, xenophobic themes in American popular and academic culture. Psychology as a whole was sometimes depicted as under threat from internal and external enemies. This fear was relayed through the images and allusions which make up the subtext of reviews of the progress of psychology. One striking illustration is in the 1937 Golden Jubilee Volume of the *American Journal of Psychology*. The editor described the first 'invasion' into psychology of 'immig-rant subjects' and the threatened 'adulteration' of positivism after the war:

> Then before experimentation and other sound methods could counter, came the Second Invasion to substitute easy and absorbing narrations of disorder, childhood sex, and personality in terms of herding instinct, id, ego, libido, repression, conflict, the unconscious, and the lurid doctrine of lust in little children. (Bentley 1937: 61)

When the events of such a wide stretch of time are rendered in narrative form, the paradoxes start to reappear as ironies. It does seem odd that psychology should use the rhetorics of race and nationhood when it had taken such care to insulate itself from the culture (as represented in pragmatist philosophy and sociology), and had attempted to insulate its beloved rational, autonomous, individualized 'subjects' in the laboratories from the outside social world. Of course, as new paradigm critics of laboratory-experimentation were to point out, it is impossible to escape 'confounding variables' by shutting out everything. If you do this you end up simply re-recording over and over the effects of a bizarre social situation (Harré and Secord 1972).

These paradoxes are not simply ironies, however. The differences reflect conflicts inside and outside psychology, and then conflicts inside and outside social psychology. The differences could be usefully viewed as ironic 'textual' matters (and I will suggest how we might go about this in the following chapters), but they must always also be located in power relations and resistance to power. The question then is, what is it that resists?

Agency and behaviour

The easy option would be to defend the individual 'subject' against the designs of the experimenter. I use the term 'subject' here to refer both to the subject ('s') in the experiment who attempts to interact with the experimenter ('E') *and* the subject ('being') of philosophical reflection, the experience we have of our-selves. We should resist the temptation simply to defend this individual subject. That would be an appealing humanist option precisely because the subject who suffers in the experiment is intended to make exactly such an appeal. A contrast between the 'social' and the 'individual' is set up in social-psychological discourse, and the individual 'subject' is created as an 'object' of that discourse. People then talk about it (and experience it) as if it exists. To respond as good humanists would have the effect of *reinforcing* the very discourse we thought we were against (just as, for example, the anti-crowd American social psychologists strengthened the power of the demon they imagined they were exorcizing).

The key paradox in social psychology is that although it appears to defend the individual against social and collective phenomena, its traditional methodology simultaneously reduces the individual to a type of mechanism. In one sense psychology and sociology complement each other: psychology studies the individual but portrays the individual (often in behaviourist fashion) as being at the mercy of the situation; sociology studies society but is careful to set aside a space in any theoretical model for an autonomous human agent.

Social psychology perpetrates a convoluted rhetoric which at some times functions as a double-bind and at others sounds like a bad joke. As we shall see in Part two, this rhetoric has not faded progressively over the years but has been transformed as the discipline defends itself against external and internal attack. Social psychology, old and new, is structured so as to endow the individual with agency – emphasize the person's 'attitudes', respect 'beliefs', and study each set of 'attributions' – but to do this by stripping the individual of any control. Individuals are made powerless through their participation in a laboratory experiment where they have no rights to alter the rules, or in a field experiment where they are the unwitting players in a setting they must necessarily misunderstand.

Power and truth

The consequences of the paradoxical rhetoric of social psychology for radicals are threefold. The first is to do with the nature of power itself. I have already moved from an individualistic, tra-ditional view of power to one which takes account of the way institutional structures (both practical and expressive) place people in positions of control or helplessness. We now have to take this further and explore how the 'power-subject' experiences that position: what is the nature of that subjectivity. In our history of laboratory-experimental social psychology, the subjectivity which emerges is one which includes themes of being observed, being powerless, and being responsible: the subject is invited to imagine that power is absent because it is hidden deep within themselves (Foucault 1981).

The second consequence is that we are empowered to see how social psychology arose to capitalize on these extra dimensions of power. We can go further than this, to say that social psychology was of a piece with the social, political, and economic changes which brought about a new subjectivity, a subjectivity necessarily caught in meshes of power from the moment it comes into being. The history of social psychology illustrates how power and resistance work when we move outside the traditional accounts and attend to conflicts outside academic boundaries. The discourse of social psychology is connected with the discourses of the surrounding culture, and all such modern discourses 'subject' the individual (Parker 1988a).

The third and final consequence is that the descriptions of the different discourses which intersected at the point we now call 'social psychology' are descriptions of a historical period which we are *now* in a position to call 'modernity'. Modernity is the cultural form dominant in the western world for the past century and a half which encourages us to represent the world as if it were organized by metanarratives of humanized science, progress, and individual meaning. My position on this has been made easier to adopt because that modern culture appears to be breaking down. There are spaces of resistance opened up by *post*modernity (Lyotard 1984). (I will explore this possibility in Chapter seven.)

Politics

This political history of social psychology has concentrated on America because that is where the discipline, as we understand it in America and in most of the English-speaking world, began. I have brought the question of class to the fore in my descriptions of the resistance and defeats which made the discipline possible, but there are other shared lines of oppression which we who are outside America share with those inside. The assumptions ground into the laboratory-experimental 'paradigm' have also conditioned perceptions by social psychologists of possible alternatives. The assumptions then deceive critics who would like something better.

All of this baggage has been exported and linked into societies in Europe and the Third World no less oppressively. We have to deal with that history of the discipline which has been made our history before we can construct real alternatives.

The political repercussions continue to the present day, and the politics I will discuss in Chapter eight will have to address issues of cultural dominance in the discipline. The power American social psychology has enjoyed has had much to do with economic power. Glossier, cheaper textbooks, more laboratories, and more men have enabled it to lead the world. This point also flows into another issue to do with social psychology as a gendered discipline, and the links between a 'hard' science obsessed with 'seminal' papers and penetrating arguments, and the nature of those who staff it. Alternatives have to address the discourse, the expressive power of the discipline, as well as its practice.

The political consequences of this understanding of the paradoxical discourses which make up 'modern' culture are, not surprisingly, difficult to articulate in the terminology of traditional old-paradigm social psychology. They are a little easier to understand in the language of the new paradigm, but to give these issues a more powerful voice I will now turn to the language of post-structuralism and post-structuralist accounts of language.

Chapter three

The conceptual crisis

Transformations in the economic and political structure of American society changed the nature of social inquiry. We have seen in the previous chapter how social psychology emerged as an experimental science, and how that science supported a particular image of the human subject. This chapter shows that the essential characteristics of those transformations were repetitions of cultural shifts in European culture around a century earlier. The transformations also carried with them conceptual changes – mutations in thought – which meant that the images of the 'subjects' of social psychology when it was born were complementary to their lived experience in the surrounding culture.

The notion of 'modernity' is useful here, for it refers to the culture which prioritizes individual meaning, the human sciences, and notions of progress. I will discuss this more fully further on when I come to Foucault's (1970) work. In brief, modernity is contradictory: its discourse promises scientific truth as the solution to humanity's problems on the one hand, and on the other attributes responsibility and the power to make meaning to individuals. In social psychology, then, we have both a mechanistic study of behaviour which suffocates human agency *and* an individualistic notion of rationality which is predicated upon that agency. This contradiction is often expressed in psychology in the heated debates between those who advocate a positivist and those who champion a phenomenological approach to the explanation of action.

This contradiction which makes up the modern age has been pursued further in the developments outside traditional social psychology traced in this chapter, developments social psychology has, until the paradigm shift, resolutely ignored. Positivism – a 'scientific' method for the understanding of the laws of societies and individuals – found a new sophisticated voice in structuralism, and phenomenology – by which I mean the study of the meanings of human experience – was further refined by practitioners of hermeneutics.

As we saw in Chapter one, both structuralism and hermeneutics have been represented in ethogenic new social psychology: structuralism in the work of Rom Harré (1979); and hermeneutics in the writings of John Shotter (1984). The picture is really slightly more complicated than this because each writer also draws upon the other's ideas to supplement his own. As we shall see, this is part of the logic of the relationship between the two conceptual poles. Because both positions represent aspects of modernity, and are defined by way of the other, neither can offer a solution to the 'crisis' inside or outside social psychology. Each requires the other and folds into the other under pressure.

In the course of this chapter I will briefly show what structuralism offered and why it failed, and then turn to developments outside social psychology which have gone beyond positivism vs. phenomenology and structuralism vs. hermeneutic dichotomies to take up the texts of post-structuralism.

Structuralism, semiology, and hermeneutics

While experimental social psychology was making its entrance before the First World War in America, Ferdinand de Saussure was asserting in Central Europe that

> *A science that studies the life of signs within society* is conceivable; it would be a part of social psychology and consequently of general psychology; I shall call it *semiology* (from the Greek *sēmeîon* 'sign'). Semiology would show what constitutes signs, what laws govern them. (Saussure 1974: 16)

The reconstruction of Saussure's lecture notes containing this suggestion for a new 'science' did not refer to 'structures' (Saussure preferred to speak of 'systems' of signs), nor was language supposed to be the key to the new science (Saussure argued that linguistics would be but 'a part' of semiology). Nevertheless, Saussure became retrospectively dubbed the father of 'structural linguistics', of structuralism, and his 'science that studies the life of signs' effectively became a part of social psychology during the paradigm revolution in the discipline some sixty years after his work. The three key components of Saussure's structuralism are his descriptions of signs, his strictures on relations, and his understanding of the role of rules in the system.

Signs

It is possible to define signs in the context of what Harré (1979) calls the expressive order of society without ever referring to the practical sphere. This first point is one which makes new social psychology a properly semiological enterprise. Its main concern is with the organization of shared meanings. Signs have two components, combining a spoken sound image (or inscription) and a concept. So, for example, if someone uses the term 'social psychologist', they are uttering or writing a sequence of sounds or patterns. This is the signifier of the sign 'social psychologist'. Glued to that signifier is the concept or commonly understood notion of what a social psychologist is. That notion is the signified. If you were to overhear a group of sociologists at a party discussing experimental social psychology, the sign 'social psychologist' might waft around, and you might feel that the concept (or signified) they share when they voice the term (or signifier) bears no relation to the actual referent, to a real social psychologist. In fact, it need bear no such relation to the real to be a sign, and to study the 'life of signs' you need not be concerned with real things at all.

Saussure argued that the connection between the signifier and signified is arbitrary. So, when you talk about social psychologists in a little social world of social psychologists, you may understand something entirely different from what your auntie thinks they are up to when she discusses it with her colleagues in the literature department. You might see how the arbitrariness of the connection between signifier and signified gives rise to a struggle for meaning at the interface of social worlds or speech communities; for example, you will, perhaps, have had to place a different, and more appropriate, auntie signified under the written signifier 'auntie' during the course of reading the previous sentence.

New social psychology steps inside the small social worlds it studies, and, using the accounts of participants, attempts to elucidate the 'life of signs' in those worlds. Unlike behaviourist experimental social psychologists, who stick to the measurement of movements, the 'new paradigm' works upwards to take account of their function as actions, and to discover their meanings as acts. One of the reasons ethogenics adopted the stance of participant observation is its belief that only then can the researcher treat the signs as they are actually used and understood (with the signifiers and the signifieds appropriately glued together).

Relations

For new social psychologists, it is an axiom of their approach that meaning is shared. It is not possible to understand the meaning of any component sign without understanding the others: in language 'there are only differences *without positive terms*' (Saussure 1974: 120). Meaning is dependent on differences and similarities with other meanings. So, for example, the often cited ethogenic study of Oxford United football supporters outlined the meanings of the systems of regalia worn on the terraces (Marsh, Rosser, and Harré 1974). A scarf has a particular meaning as a sign, and would call into being for an observer the idea of the category of fan who was wearing it. It also brings into play a whole range of meanings and relationships through connotation. The scarf carries meaning as a sign by virtue of its relations with other items of clothing, not because the signified is in some magical way woven into the wool.

There are two ways to look at the relations in a sign system. First, there is a range of possible alternatives that can be *selected*: a football supporter may choose to wear a scarf instead of a cravat; a social psychologist may chose a qualitative field study instead of a laboratory experiment. (Remember that we are concerned here simply with the meaning of the items chosen, not their practical value.) Second, the signs can be *combined* in different ways: a football supporter may wear the scarf round his waist or his wrist; a social psychologist may display her 'data' as observed facts at the beginning of a report to be accounted for, or illustrations of a theoretical position at the conclusion of an article to provide confirmation.

For new social psychology, the selection of signs and their combinations by a social actor also carry with them the self-presentations of persons within their own community. The choice of an inappropriate item of clothing by a football fan or an unacceptable research procedure by a social psychologist has to be warranted; it has to be explained to the satisfaction of other members of the community. At the same time, with that warrant comes the awareness that others are obtaining concepts (signifieds) of the type of person you are which are embedded in the accounts (signifiers) you offer them. So, a football fan reconstructs and lives the image of a 'novice' or 'nutter' depending on his clothing and actions; and a social psychologist will have to struggle to redefine and avoid the image of a hard-faced behaviourist or a woolly humanist, depending on the methods she adopts.

Rules

The reconstruction of the system of signs circulating in a chosen social world on the basis of accounts gathered from members is a difficult business. In part, the difficulty arises from the fact that at some point the researcher will have to step beyond the knowledge displayed by one individual to a shared social knowledge, the system of meanings and rules, which will only have a *collective* existence.

The step beyond the consciousness of the individual 'subject', and back from the personal meanings held by the members of a community, is necessary if the researcher is to engage in a 'science' of signs. There is, structuralists believe, an underlying reality – of real structures – which underpins and organizes particular observable manifestations. The total system or 'structure' is what Saussure called language, and the individual items which a researcher will piece together he called speech. New social psychology employed a slightly different terminology to capture the same distinction but talk of a distinction between 'performance' (Saussure's 'speech') and 'competence' (*almost* equivalent to the underlying structure) instead (Harré and Secord 1972). The work of the ethogenist, it is claimed, is to attend to the performances of individuals in order to arrive at their underlying competence. This latter distinction implies that the underlying knowledge is possessed by each and every individual. Saussure did also claim that each item of language was present in every head, but in practice structuralism (and new social psychology) has worked on the assumption that the 'competence' or 'language' is a collective property. Society members contribute to social knowledge, ethogenics argues, as pieces of a jigsaw to make a whole picture.

It follows from semiological descriptions of meaning and structure in language that a historical study of items of meaning must be read with extreme care. Saussure drew a distinction between an analysis which would be concerned with the historical evolution of a system, and a properly semiological analysis which would be concerned with the nature of a structure at any given time. New social psychology has concentrated on the task of elaborating structures of meaning as they exist at the moment they are studied. It has deliberately restricted its focus, carrying out intensive studies of a specific football ground or school. It would, of course, make a nonsense of the whole structuralist project to imagine that the history of an individual sign could tell us much about its present-day meaning. Nevertheless, it is possible, as we shall see below when we turn to Foucault's (1970) work, to develop some overall 'history' of mutations from one cultural system to another. This notion of change, however, which deliberately devalues the history of meanings which could be given by individuals, also threatens to reinforce the 'scientific' character of structuralism. We are led to believe that there is a social knowledge – or meaning – which, of its nature, escapes and *determines* the individual 'subject'.

Hermeneutics

There is a sense in which the scientific pretensions of structuralism are just another twist to the positivism which informed the mechanistic enterprise of experimental social psychology. Structuralism's notorious 'anti-humanism' follows logically on from the belief that systems of meaning operate despite individual intention, and determine the thoughts, acts, and actions of human agents. However, there is a deeper sense in which structuralism also represents, at a theoretical level, the webs of modernity of which experimental social psychology is a mere thread. It is paradoxical and dualistic in the way experimental social psychology is: social action is reduced to measured movements, but individual responsibility is attributed to the 'subject'. It holds within itself the carefully delimited space for intention and agency to thrive. Who 'selects' signs from the paradigmatic and syntagmatic axes of language but the subject? Structuralism paradoxically requires, even more explicitly than its positivist predecessors, the individual as a supplement to its mechanistic account. This individual aspect is provided by hermeneutics.

Hermeneutics was originally the study of biblical texts, and practitioners aimed to recover from those texts a true meaning imagined to be the word of God. Now hermeneutics in social science turns on the meanings within texts which are placed there by human agents. Although some recent developments in the approach work with the notion of a 'social text' with meanings that cannot be traced to the intentions of individuals, it still, by and large, rests on the belief that the meaning of human activities can be made open, transparent, and understandable to all (Shotter 1983).

I have concentrated so far, in my account of new social psychology, on the more structuralist version which derives from *The Explanation of Social Behaviour* (Harré and Secord 1972) and which is carried through in the writings of Harré, to the exclusion of the hermeneutics to be found in *Human Action and its Psychological Investigation* (Gauld and Shotter 1977) and in the writings of Shotter. There are fairly extensive disagreements between them with many ramifications which I will return to again in Part two of this book.

We can touch just briefly on the disagreements here. Take, for example, Harré's assertion that 'Pattern, convention and rule emerge even in the apparently most inhumane or most casual social surroundings. The tendency to identify co-ordinated social action with co-operative, altruistic action is a sentimentality and should be avoided' (Harré 1979: 70). He goes on to trace the bases of social structure to 'cognitive templates', and in this way, paradoxically, threatens to collapse his structuralist social account into an individualistic explanation of action. Now compare this with the complaint from the hermeneutic side of the new social psychology that Harré's idea of social 'grammars' located in people's heads is a 'threat to self and genuine individuality' (Shotter 1980: 52).

Harré's version of new social psychology is also closer to structuralism when it appeals to underlying structures with causal powers. Shotter, on the other hand, prefers to stick to the surface as a general rule to avoid imagining there is something 'behind' meaningful human action. In recent years this has led him to a position he characterizes as 'mundane realism' (Shotter 1984).

The differences between the two wings of new social psychology are important for two reasons: they highlight the problem of scientism in the structuralist approach: and they demonstrate the dualism which lies hidden in the 'new paradigm' alternative to the explicitly dualistic 'old paradigm' experimental social psychology. Although the new social psychology provides valuable criticisms of experimentation, it does not escape the polarity of mechanistic positivist science and individual phenonomenological experience which is a conceptual reflection of the modern age. It is trapped within a representation of the world as organized by the meta-narratives of humanized science, progress, and individual meaning. Structuralism, then, which appears to produce a watertight positivist account of the laws and rules of meaning is actually contradictory. It holds within its own structure the intentionalism of hermeneutics. We should now turn to the way the contradictions in structuralism have been explored and deconstructed by *post*-structuralists.

The contexts of post-structuralism

The political ferment in and around Paris in 1968 affected all academic life. Radicals who were involved in the protest movements started to question the ideological function of the human (and natural) sciences, and liberals who had long been uneasy with the order of things in their disciplines found a space to air their grievances. While the political projects of the Left failed, the period around 1968 saw huge cracks appear in the cultural superstructure of the system they fought. This superstructure – modernity – came under threat in different disciplines in different ways. Modern laboratory-experimental social psychology was disrupted by a conceptual 'crisis' which threw up the new social psychologists influenced by Saussurean ideas hoping to reform it, but outside the discipline, structuralism was already under attack.

Structuralism promised a science of language in work on literature (Barthes 1977), a science of society in anthropology (Lévi-Strauss 1966), and a science of modes of production in politics (Althusser 1971). The hope was that this scientific approach would produce an objective explanation of societal and personal phenomena. At the end of the 1960s, however, this dehumanizing revamp of positivism came under attack by some who wanted to

revive humanism (in the guise of phenomenology or hermeneutics), and, more radically, those who wanted to go beyond both
structuralism and humanism. This was the context for the publication of a number of wide-ranging critiques of the modern human
sciences by Jacques Derrida (1973, 1976, 1978). Derrida's work
could provide social psychologists with useful ways of thinking
about texts and suggestions on the 'deconstruction' of social
psychology's texts. It will also, despite post-structuralist opposition to the term, help us to grapple with the problem of *ideology*.

Texts

Pieces of writing called 'texts' normally promise to do two things,
and, correspondingly, can be read in two ways. The first is to do
with the ostensible function of a text to represent some state of
affairs by providing a written summary of information about a
particular topic. We are invited to believe that when we read
Milgram's (1963) experimental social psychology text about obedience, for example, the introduction, table of results, and conclusion will re-present for us the essence of 'obedience'. Social
psychology textbooks integrate this knowledge with findings on
other topics such as 'attraction' or 'prejudice' and dish it up with
some general nostrums about social interaction. These too, then,
pretend to represent a reality outside the text. A powerful,
culturally determined distinction between what is written and what
is 'real' is at work here. A correlative assumption is that we can
check the veracity of texts by sampling reality for ourselves.

Another way to read a text is to treat it as the carefully wrought
thought of the writer. The text can, we suppose, be interpreted, and
supplemented with information about the author, to reveal other
deeper, and more accurate, meanings. Social psychologists have,
traditionally, been less interested in this. They have been concerned
with the real world rather than real intentions of writers. This process
of interpretation has been pursued more extensively within literature: it is a variety of hermeneutics. However, the premise is once
again that the text represents what is outside the text, and that we
can hold to a distinction between the written and the real. If this
were true we could go to the author and ask what was really
meant. A cluster of problems, ranging from mortality and memory
to self-presentation, makes this an impossible endeavour.

New social psychology also trades in this distinction, and its use of structuralism retains a notion of a reality which is represented in its texts. Ethogenic researchers, for example, gathered football supporters' explanations of their activities and produced an account which purported to represent the real meanings of the football-terrace community. In structuralist parlance, they captured the 'signifieds' held within the signs circulating in the social world studied, discovered the relations between them, and reconstructed the shared system of rules which made up the language of that world. Ethogenic texts, then, pretend to represent what their subjects really mean.

However, texts are tissues of meaning which have powers to weave new pictures of the real every time they are read or re-read. If it is true, as Saussure claimed, that in language there are only *differences* and no 'positive terms', then it would not be possible to capture a 'true', positive, meaning. Derrida (1976) takes this further and argues that each attempt to move beyond a text to find the true meaning is doomed, for the study of the outside is a *reading* which is given meaning by a context.

The context effectively operates as another text, hence the well-known phrase *'there is nothing outside of the text'* (Derrida 1976: 158). Texts, then, do re-present meanings, but those meanings are transformed meanings from other texts, and the meanings change across situations and over time. The implications of this line of argument for a scientific structuralism are dire, since it would make the recovery of 'true' meanings and 'structures' impossible. Texts should now be defined as delimited tissues of meaning which may be written, spoken, or reproduced in *any form* that can be given an interpretative gloss.

Deconstruction

Traditional notions of the text 'work' by privileging what is outside the text – as the container of the real – over the text itself. The text merely represents it. This opposition between what is 'true' and what is not is one of the many metaphysical oppositions Derrida reveals and overturns in his deconstructions of western thought. Deconstruction could be characterized as one process by which we can expose and subvert the restriction of meaning in a text. It might be tempting to think of deconstruction merely as a method.

We should resist this temptation, though for simplicity's sake I will run through three possible steps to a deconstruction of meaning in a text.

For Derrida, one of the exemplars of a metaphysical opposition which restricts meaning, and which deludes us into imagining that there is a single true meaning to be found, is that between speech and writing. Traditionally, we understand speech to be closer to thought than writing. As we speak, we appear to be putting thoughts into words as if we were filling them with meaning, and as we hear ourselves speak it is as if we were hearing our thoughts. Writing, on the other hand, seems more obviously mediated and is liable to read in different ways in different contexts.

The first step to a deconstruction is to identify just such an opposition, and to show how one of the terms (in this case, speech) is dominant in the truth stakes over the other (in this case, writing). There are other issues in this particular example, for the privilege speech is accorded over writing helps guarantee the sovereignty of the autonomous person – the idealized individual much beloved of western thought in general, and of social psychology in particular. New social psychology, which is sympathetic to individualist humanist arguments, reinforces the distinction between speech and writing every time it inveighs against the use of questionnaires or documents in favour of 'asking people' and gathering 'real' accounts (Harré 1981a).

The second step is to subvert the opposition between the two terms by demonstrating that the privilege the dominant term enjoys can be made untenable. In many respects, for example, speech undergoes the same sort of vicissitudes as writing between being produced by one person and received by another. When we are speaking we do not have complete control over what we say. Instead, we are at the mercy of a language which is filled with meanings that we have, in a sense, to borrow and reproduce when we use it. Language is gendered, and it is also organized to restrict the experience of those outside the dominant culture. Standard English suppresses working-class speech and dialect (and the reader who doubts this should attempt to deliver a paper to a social psychology conference in something other than middle-class form). Speech accommodation also reproduces different categories of speech style and boundaries between what is acceptable and who should be discounted. Within social groups, certain names, terms, and phrases may be reserved for those who have rights to speak. In many ways, then, speech is a specially woven tissue and it operates as if it were a variety of writing.

The third step of deconstruction involves the sabotaging of the conceptual opposition. This can be done by extending the meaning of the term 'writing' to include what we commonly label 'speech'. Alternatively, we could employ a different term which would prevent the opposition from reasserting itself. In the present case, we would want to do this because we want to expose structures of coercion in language; and in order to do that we have to resist the comfortable myth that there is a space for unmediated, genuine communication between people which is free from the operation of power. Two things can be drawn out of the third step of deconstruction in this context. The first is conceptual, and the second practical.

First, take one of the conceptual fruits of Derrida's work on speech and writing. There is a term which would apply to both, and which would render them open to a critical study. This is the term which signals that *all* investigation is mediated by socially shared and culturally constructed meanings. If this account is correct, then, as I pointed out at the beginning of Chapter one, even such a seemingly 'natural' experience as direct perception is impossible. The term is one we have already discussed and defined earlier in this chapter – 'text'. The work deconstruction can accomplish for us, then, is to open up texts to show how meaning is organized and what function that organization serves. We can use it to show what interpretations are powerful, and then we can explore how and why they enjoy that power. In this sense deconstruction can be one useful conceptual weapon in the struggle against ideology.

Second, there are political consequences which flow from a deconstruction. It would be possible to think of American and European social psychology as two pairs of an opposition, or the old paradigm and new paradigm as opposing approaches. I opened up the conflict between the warring sides as the first deconstructive step, and I championed European social psychology and supported the new paradigm as the second step. Out of the wreckage, however, should come something entirely different. A successful deconstruction of social psychology would end it, and in its place we would have alternative understandings of subjectivity and social relations based in politics. *Politics* (a critical view of power and ideology, and support for resistance and conflict) emerges as the third term as social psychology falls away. However, because such a deconstruction would be tackling an academic *institution*, and not just a set of concepts, we have to link the practical measures (at the end of Chapter eight) to our unravelling of the way it functions expressively, ideologically.

Ideology

There are two unhelpful ways to describe ideology. One is to say that ideology is simply a system of beliefs. This definition of ideology is the one often adopted in mainstream sociology. In social psychology it has recently, to all intents and purposes, reappeared in the research on 'social representations' (as you will see in Chapter five). The disadvantage of this position is that we lose any critical edge in our use of the term. We need to retain some conception of ideology as being restrictive or coercive in its effects. It renders invisible the operations of power, and nowhere more so than when we are led to accept that it is a necessary glue which holds people together. Both structuralism and post-structuralism unfortunately tend to advocate a thorough-going relativism which invalidates everything (including oppositional arguments), and thus effectively could just as well be condoning everything. For political reasons I want to keep some distance from Derrida's (and Foucault's) hostility to the term 'ideology'.

The other, less unhelpful, way of describing ideology is to say that it is a system of illusion or lies. If this were the case then it could easily be dispelled by asserting truth. The problem with this position is that, as far as social interaction is concerned, we face insurmountable difficulties in saying what the truth is. It may be possible to discover larger-scale laws in economics, or to display inequalities of income and opportunity in sociology, but as we narrow our focus on to the smaller-scale domains held together by texts, nearly every account of social life can, to some extent, be contested. Post-structuralist notions of the text throw into question the possibility of arriving at a definitive true meaning, and, further, offer a critique of 'truth' as such. Nevertheless, post-structuralism helps us demystify the 'truth' in the dominant culture, and is politically useful if it is turned to that task.

Theories of ideology have invariably trodden a tortuous path between these two positions and have usually fallen into the one side or the other. They have slipped, I believe, when they have attempted to give a definition of ideology, or to set out criteria which could be used to identify it. It is more useful to keep resisting the temptation to refer to ideology as a thing. It is not a property of social meaning, but a label which identifies the coercive function of meaning in specific contexts. The criteria for using the term ideology do not rest in the object to be discovered but in the power of the subjects who are in conflict with it. It becomes salient when we can ask what sets of statements *do* and what institutional restrictive functions those statements serve.

A deconstructive reading, as defined by Derrida (1981), is an ally of such a critical stance towards ideology which does not appeal to a truth outside the text:

> the reading must always aim at a certain relationship, unperceived by the writer, between what he [sic] commands and what he does not command of the patterns of the language that he uses. This relationship is not a certain quantitative distribution of shadow and light, of weakness or of force, but a signifying structure that critical reading should *produce*. (Derrida 1976: 158)

Ideology should be a function of politically charged rhetoric. This politics takes form when we bring in notions of history, power, and resistance.

Contradictions

Notwithstanding Derrida's warning that we cannot move outside the text, we have to refer to the 'real' in some way in order to provide an adequate account of power and the development of different forms of power in different cultures. When we are dealing with small-scale social interaction in a particular culture, however, it is pointless and hopeless to appeal to reality. The understanding we can give of the social and historical status of different texts should, then, be informed by our understanding of the role of discourse.

Discourse

A discourse is a system of statements which constructs an object. This fictive object will then be reproduced in the various texts written or spoken within the domain of discourses (that is, within the expressive order of society). So, for example, social psychologists may draw upon a discourse of 'authoritarianism' and they will use the notion of 'authoritarianism', which has been constructed as an object by that discourse, to explain different social and political phenomena. Each time they use the term they will, by the same token, be reproducing the discourse. We find academic or popular texts circulating which draw upon and support that discourse. Another example, referred to in Chapter two, is the discourse relating to 'the crowd'. The obsessive attempts to combat the effects of, or even the idea of, the 'crowd mind' paradoxically reproduced the discourse. Many texts, such as Le Bon's (1896) book, drew upon that discourse.

Foucault attempted, in historical research first published in France during the 1960s, to show how particular systems of discourse affected western culture. Paradoxically, his influential book *The Order of Things*, which was popularly understood to be the bible of structuralism, was actually an account of how structuralism came about as a contradictory component of modernity (Foucault 1970). The book described overarching structures of discourse – termed *epistemes* – which determine what it is possible to speak of, and think (though there will always be some swimming against the stream). The *epistemes* (or epistemological structures) are wider-ranging than Kuhn's (1970) paradigms, and the mutations which create and destroy them are not necessarily historically progressive.

The *epistemes* are described (rather too conveniently) by Foucault as lasting roughly 150 years each. We should be extremely cautious about adopting these time windows as rigid schemas, but they can help us to pick out dominant cultural preoccupations. The Renaissance, for example, was governed by a symbolist view of the world and language which encouraged interpretation aimed at recovering an ultimate meaning of things in the true word of God. His signature was everywhere, and hermeneutics was in full flower. This epistemological configuration mutated in the middle of the seventeenth century into the Classical Age. Now rationalism reigned, and natural science proved a (mechanistic) model for ordering the world and language to give a true picture. It was in this climate that the French *idéologues* thought they could accurately represent thought and so dispel illusion (Billig 1982).

Mechanistic approaches did not entirely disappear at the close of the eighteenth century, but the production of meaning and knowledge started to be attributed to individual human beings at the dawn of the Modern Age. While the Classical Age developed themes of representation, the Modern Age, modernity, focused attention on the individual, for the individual was seen as responsible for producing that representation. At stake now was not only the representation of the real world but also the representation of meaning. The twin aspects of the contradictory meaning of the verb 'to represent', which came with the term when it appeared in the English language four centuries earlier, now found cultural support: 'to represent' was to make present to the mind *and* to stand for something which is not present. In modernity, the human being was not only the clarifier of true meaning, but its producer, its centre. Now psychology, and social psychology, could be born (Parker 1988a).

Discipline

In modernity, human agency is a valuable commodity, and humanist sentiments are, at first sight, progressive. Foucault goes on to show, however, that the belief that individuals are endowed with the ability to produce meaning, truth, is a trap. The human being is seen as both the object and also the subject of understanding. Foucault's later work described how although this paradox may be a mere academic puzzle to philosophers and psychologists, it is an unpleasant lived experience for inhabitants of the modern world. 'Subjects' in modernity are fixed in place from without by apparatuses of discipline (Foucault 1977), and from within by processes of confession (Foucault 1981).

The traditional way in which power is defined in social science is as the exercise of one person's will over others. As we saw in Chapter two, however, this conception of power is inadequate when put to the test. It may have been appropriate up to the end of the eighteenth century (though even then it would not account for everything) when the paradigm case would be the exercise of the will of the monarch against the body of the criminal in public punishments and executions. We can dub this type of power 'sovereign' power. The transition to modernity, however, was accompanied by the elaboration of mechanisms of surveillance and control which transformed the operation of power within society and between people. Foucault (1977) refers to the rise in population, the concentration of production, and the emergency control measures adopted to deal with the Plague as practical springs for the transition to this type of power.

There is a model form described by Foucault (1977) which captures the essential aspects of the new disciplinary power. In the Panopticon there is a central guard tower which is circled by cells which are backlit so every activity of the prisoner can be seen. The prisoners cannot see the guards, for the crucial point is that they should believe themselves to be seen. The deliberate exercise of intended effects is not necessary, then, for power to operate. The subjects of power can do the work themselves. If you have ever been the subject in a social psychology experiment (or even in an interview project accounting for your actions) you will know what this experience is like. It is not accidental that social-psychological research provides a good example of how disciplinary power works. Were its many and varied projects carried out, you would not even be able to go to the toilet without feeling you were being watched.

Within institutions, the control apparatuses and the mechanisms of surveillance had the function of regulating behaviour and identifying abnormalities and pathologies. Each person was encouraged to look within to discover their faults and flaws. Along with discipline, then, went the process of confession which gave a new modern twist to notions of individuality. (The concept of an 'I' and the production of autobiographies appeared in Europe in the twelfth century.) The idea that a truth exists deep within the person, which may be held down by power and which may be liberated through confession, is one of the individualist myths of modern culture. If we experience difficulty in finding this truth (a truth which has, in addition, been increasingly sexualized), we become all the more convinced that it is the more deeply repressed. Thus 'it is in the confession that truth and sex are joined, through the obligatory and exhaustive expression of an individual secret' (Foucault 1981: 61).

Power

The notions of discipline and confession are descriptive devices designed to illuminate power, and they serve as theoretical points of *resistance* to that power. To use the terms 'discipline' and 'confession' is to indict the key opposition which makes up modernity *and* which is hidden inside the project of structuralism. On the one hand, positivist and behaviourist attempts to quantify and reduce human action to units of behaviour and to regulate that behaviour (for example, in old social psychology) function as a disciplinary power. On the other hand, the attribution of responsibility and agency to the individual subjects (and in new social psychology the giving of 'rights' to account for their actions) can function complementarily as incitement to confess. Power not only constrains and excludes; it is also productive. Just as discourse produces objects or topics of investigation, it also produces *subjects*.

Laboratory-experimental social psychology was built as a disciplinary apparatus. New social psychology emphasizes individual accounts, but instead of escaping power, it participates in the correlative mechanisms of confession. New social psychology does expose the mechanistic character of the discipline and (as a reflection of explicitly structuralist ideas) is more open to the developments in the theory of language offered by post-structuralism, but the continuing crisis in social psychology is part of broader cultural and political crises. This means that in order to realize the critical potential of new social psychology we have had to add a sense of its historical position. Now the crisis could be transformed from being simply a condition of uncertainty and suspense into a turning-point. To accomplish that involves putting to work analyses of power and ideology.

The idea of power we can develop from this work is one which is concerned with the reproduction of relations between people in which resistance is suppressed. It does not rest on the intention of a power-holder, and so it is possible to give an account which situates it in the operation of discourses and texts. A deconstruction applied to those texts, then, necessarily starts to unravel the power relations which hold them in place. What we understand to be ideology and conflict in the course of revealing power and resistance are the *effects* of those relations in discourses and texts. Ideology is not a thing.

Post-structuralists (and Foucault has been particularly vocal on this score) are right to say that when we use the term ideology we risk understating the power of the truth which holds disciplines together in this culture, and we risk setting up a truth as an alternative to the lies we have exposed. As will have been quite clear so far, I do not agree that those risks should lead us to abandon the term. When I use the term politically, I am concerned not with what it refers to, but with what it *does* and what institutional conflicts it brings into play. To talk of ideology in the deconstruction of texts and discourses is to support resistance. This is the whole point of taking the paradigm revolution in social psychology into the realms of post-structuralism.

Part two

Responses

New social psychology is both an opportunity and a danger to those of us who want to develop radical ideas in the human sciences. It is useful in so far as it opens up the contradictions between mechanistic studies of behaviour (exemplified in positivist approaches) and the attribution of intention to autonomous agents (found in psychology's methodological individualism). New social psychology also echoes the tension outside the discipline between structuralism and hermeneutics. Here is the opportunity, for the debates in the paradigm crisis literature focus on the role of language in reproducing social relations. The door has been pushed open for the discussion of power and ideology in social-psychological discourses and texts.

The danger lies in the role that new social psychology plays as a loyal opposition within the discipline. The double demand of such a role is that it both challenges *and* buttresses social psychology as an institution. This neglects the way the paradigm crisis also provoked *traditional* social psychology into taking language seriously. Over the last fifteen years the old regime has taken measures to absorb ethogenic critiques, taking on board some of their ideas, and to mould experimental methodology to meet changing conditions in the real world.

Traditional social psychology is clueless when it comes to the cultural and political context of its research, and wilfully dismissive of its place in the reproduction of ideology and power. It answers criticisms only in order to strengthen itself. More disturbing still is the way it shifts towards the new social psychology positions just enough to bring them back within the fold – to recuperate them and to dilute the force of their arguments. The theoretical and methodological refinements of recent years appear to be genuine responses, but they are actually ingenious *reactions*. They are defences which immobilize the opposition, to pretend there is no longer a crisis.

Part two of this book is concerned with three such defensive measures on the part of traditional social psychology: the turn to 'ordinary explanations', which promises to carry attribution theory outside the laboratory and take what people say in good faith; the theory of 'social representations', which claims to borrow from the best of sociology and to reveal the content of a social shared reality; and ethnomethodology, which appears to support the study of texts and to account for the construction of conversation and rhetoric. Each of these three approaches connects with ethogenic notions and each has been enthusiastically welcomed, to varying degrees, by new social psychologists. Each, however, finally fails to deal with issues of coercion and control in society and social life.

In Chapters four, five and six then, I discuss case studies of developments in social psychology which have occurred as a direct result of the paradigm crisis in the discipline (the research on 'ordinary explanations'); which owe something to the political crisis which conditioned the paradigm debates (writings on 'social representations'); and one of which explicitly addresses post-structuralist outcomes of the conceptual crisis running parallel to the crisis in other human sciences (the work on ethnomethodology).

In each chapter I take a corpus of texts – those delimited tissues of meaning which develop the theory or report the appropriate evidence – treating them as contributions to overarching discourses. These discourses are the systems of statements which construct objects (which here are those things we recognize to be 'ordinary explanations', 'social representations', or 'conversations').

In Chapter four I subject the discourse of attribution theory to a deconstruction, that is, I expose and subvert the restriction of meaning in the texts which comprise it. I will also show how that deconstruction can be linked with cultural changes, and how new social-psychological responses remain caught within those terms of reference. The lesson is that we must extend our use of deconstruction to account for the impact of history on social theory. Chapter five draws upon these ideas, and takes to task the discourse emerging around the theory of 'social representations'. The issues raised by deconstruction – of how the effects of power relations are relayed in discourses and texts – are glossed over. It is only possible to understand how power relations have those effects by revealing the systems of meanings which operate as *ideology*.

In Chapter six I examine the claims of the most far-reaching attempts yet within social psychology to break away from both orthodox psychology and sociology. Writers in microsociology, who have played their part in inspiring new social psychology, now seem to take on board the ideas of deconstruction and even (occasionally) talk of ideology. Their texts, however, still evade the problem of *power*, power which should be conceived of as the reproduction of relations between people in which resistance is suppressed. A recurring theme through these three chapters is that of the power of institutions, and the way that these condition texts. Chapter four is concerned with the absorption of 'ordinary explanation' into the academic institution of social psychology. Chapter five examines the effects of the split between the academic institutions of psychology and sociology on the study of everyday 'social representations'. Finally, at the close of Chapter six the institutional 'framing' of texts is described in order to counter sentimental descriptions of 'conversation' in social psychology.

Part two concludes, then, with a re-emphasis on the historically constructed institutional divisions which have permitted particular theories and practices to arise in social psychology. The purposes of these three chapters, then, are these: when we know how existing alternatives within social psychology have been neutralized we will be in a better position to ensure it does not also happen to us; we will also be better equipped to move on to explore, in Part three of the book, cultural and political options.

Chapter four

Ordinary explanation

How is it possible to construct a critique of social-psychological theory without, at some stage, endorsing the very assumptions which lie at its core? The principal problem structuralism and post-structuralism drew attention to is that the language critics use to analyse and describe the internal contradictions they discover is one they share with the proponents of the theory under attack. An additional problem is that conceptions of human action which lie at the interface of psychology and sociology inform both the tradition *and* the opposition within the disciplines. Traditional social psychology has been able, so far, to contain and neutralize its critics. In addition, our culture sustains the way most people (including social psychologists) understand and explain the distinctions between truth and opinion, science and common sense, and between the person and the social world they inhabit. This means that if we want to attack a theory, we also have to unravel the cultural webs which make it possible.

In this chapter I will show that it is possible to strike a critical distance from a theory – in this case 'attribution theory' – and to illuminate the cultural preconceptions which support it. Attribution theory purports to take seriously 'ordinary explanations' of action, and we should take that theory seriously. This discussion will involve a deconstruction of attribution theory which, together with a historical account, exposes the shortcoming of the theory as an old paradigm approach. It will also throw into question the value of the alternative voices in the new paradigm.

Attribution theory has proved to be one of the more durable and popular areas of social psychology in the last ten to fifteen years. The simple problem which guides the theory – how we discover the causal properties of social behaviour – has provoked a mass of research. Since the highpoint of its influence in the 1970s, it has extended into fields as diverse as legal studies, cross-cultural research and clinical psychology. It has also linked up with newer theoretical developments in social psychology (including the work on 'social representations' we will look at in the next chapter). On the one hand, new social psychologists have claimed that the original ideas advanced by Fritz Heider (1958) are part of their own approach (Harré 1981a). On the other hand, the old paradigm experimentalists have been able to use it to show an interest in aspects of common sense and claim that it can still be investigated quantitatively. An effect of this success has been that a common meeting-point between the 'paradigms' has been set up. The force of ethogenic criticisms of the old paradigm risks being undermined.

There have, of course, been many critiques of the theory, ethogenic ones among them. We will return to these later. Aside from some passing references to the bureaucratic rationality of contemporary life, however, new social psychology's objections have not seriously examined the historical basis of the theory, let alone the historical nature of their own alternatives. Outside the new paradigm some cultural presuppositions of the theory, and possible links with economic changes culminating in the emergence of late capitalism, have been discussed by radical social psychologists (Billig 1982). These are useful links to make if we hold on to the distinction between the practical economic order and the expressive sphere (where the stuff of social psychology is reproduced). But we still need an account of how attribution theory as well as the ethogenic alternatives have been conditioned by history.

Deconstruction will be my way of identifying and untying the conceptual structures of attribution theory. I will then be able to bring in the analysis of cultural history in the West described in Chapter three. The historical periodization offered by Foucault (1970) can throw attribution theory's assumptions about truth, science, and social behaviour into relief.

Both deconstruction, and post-structuralism generally, entail a thorough-going scepticism about truth claims. Their own position flows from the emphasis on language and is an integral part of the third perspective I want to touch on in this chapter.

Post-structuralism may have emerged when it did because the modern age has broken up to give way to a *postmodern condition*. The rapid growth of information technology and the virtual collapse of the main political reform movements of the past century are part of a fashionable, studied incertitude as to the 'real' nature of things (Lyotard 1984). People are losing faith in human science, progress, and personal meaning as 'Modern' touchstones of truth. Whether or not this is desirable as a solution to attribution theory will have to remain an open question for the present.

Attribution theory

Attribution theory has, following Heider's (1958) work on phenomenal causality in the late 1950s, been concerned with the way individuals attempt to make social life predictable and controllable. The overriding motivation thought to possess the minds of lay perceivers is that they continually strive to determine the causes for behaviour. This assumption lies at the heart of all later developments of the theory: 'The theory describes processes that operate as if the individual were motivated to attain cognitive mastery of the causal structure of his [sic] environment' (Kelley 1967: 193). The same kind of logic that is used by scientists to understand the physical world is employed by the 'naïve' actor to understand his or her social world: 'the person–perceiver's fundamental task is to interpret or infer the causal antecedents of action' (Jones and Davis 1965: 200). An observer, then, allocates causes to the external world or to other actors (and actors may attribute causes to the situation or their own selves).

These general propositions have given rise to a number of separate attribution theories. In part, the licence for this lies in the open nature of Heider's own original text. The similarity in Heider's 'naïve analysis of action' between everyday causal attribution and experimentation led Kelley (1967) to the notion of 'man [sic] the scientist'. This is a being who uses a logic analogous to that of an analysis of variance. The concern with intentionality was then developed into the idea of 'correspondent inferences' (Jones and Davis 1965). The discovery of the 'fundamental attribution error', in which actors over-attribute to situations whilst observers over-value stable personal dispositions, opened up further disputes among advocates of the theory (Jones and Nisbett 1971).

The existence of so many refinements and versions of attribution theory raises methodological issues to do with the level of analysis that should be addressed by a critic. Just as different theories are produced by different writers, so variants of the theories are present in the many formulations offered at different times by a single writer. Changes of emphasis, shifts in interest, and lapses of memory all go to produce in social psychological texts (as in all texts) a multitude of possible 'theories'. The level of analysis then finally rests on the overall theoretical orientation and aims of the analysis. It is not possible to fish out *any* interpretation. It is possible to approach the text with certain questions in mind as to its historical basis.

In this chapter the *discourse* of attribution theory is the object of study. This discourse is the overall set of statements which refer to, and so create, the phenomena of 'attributions' which we then imagine to exist within the mental apparatus of 'subjects'. This discourse includes both written and spoken texts, and I have deliberately included a paper spoken to a British psychology conference (Totman 1982) among the ethogenic responses to attribution theory. (Deconstruction does not accept that any type of text should be privileged over others, and I guess I could have made my point even more strongly by including comments made by social psychologists in the coffee bar as part of the discourse I discuss.) The sense of this discourse arises, of course, from my own selective reading of texts, and this has been informed by a set of theoretical and political concerns. The purpose is not to expose the faults of any one attribution theorist, but to dismantle and then locate the discourse of attribution theory historically. You should bear this in mind as the assumptions within the theory are outlined in the following pages.

Assumptions

The following six aspects of the theory, the assumptions which hold it together and provide the space for internal squabbles and refinements, have been discussed before by other proponents and opponents of the theory.

1: *Error*. Although people are ordinarily like scientists, they are bound to bias: 'Like all other perceptual and cognitive systems, attribution processes are subject to error' (Kelley 1967: 219). Apart from the 'fundamental attribution error', a whole field of research has developed from the attribution of causes of emotional states, into misattributions as to the meaning of arousal, and into beliefs about health. The importance of error is noted by all of those who attempt to specify exactly what type of rationality the person as 'scientist' operates with. Attribution will be worth the effort, so the story goes, 'if the perceiver's guess is correct only in a substantial fraction of cases' (Shaver 1975: 58). All of the variants of the theory specify forms of bias. The notion of error necessitates, of course, a correlative notion of hypothetically correct attributions, of truth.

2: *Relativism*. The theory takes an individual's perceptions and attributions as, for all intents and purposes, valid. This is a relativist view which flows from Heider's (1958) own stress on phenomenal causality. Some writers have argued that the development of attribution theory reflects a shift to a 'relativist logic' which is to be found in contemporary philosophy (Totman 1982). Because attribution theory does not study the 'truth' of the phenomena, but varying accounts, it accepts each person's interpretation in its own right. The actual 'cause' of the behaviour should not affect the status of the accounts. Furthermore, the experimenter's account is just one more version. Those who do not believe that the 'fundamental attribution error' is an indispensable fact of human cognition, emphasize this relativist line. Thus, one writer who takes this position argues that 'attribution theorists have no special claim to understanding reality, or even to understanding people's understanding of reality' (Harvey 1981: 302).

3: *Rationality*. The person is seen as a rational evaluator of behaviour. If Kelley were to be believed, the person is a 'scientist' employing a 'naïve' version of the 'method of differences': so Kelley claims that 'The logic of the analysis is obviously akin to that employed in analysis of variance' (Kelley 1967: 195). This scientist is an inductivist. Others have suggested that the appropriate model of the person should rather be that of a lawyer who might profit from common sense or legal notions of responsibility.

Rationalism is still a crucial feature of these accounts, though. The model of science (or the law) is used to formalize the data on behalf of the naïve 'scientist' or 'lawyer' who does not always, of course, do it properly.

4: *Common sense*. Attributions are ordinary explanations of social behaviour. An important link is thus forged with those who argued that social psychology should look to life outside the laboratory. From the earliest formulations of the theory, in which it was said that psychology had a good deal to learn from 'common-sense psychology' (Heider 1958), the focus has been on 'ordinary' judgements and decisions about causality. As Heider put it, 'Attribution is part of our cognition of the environment. Whenever you cognize your environment you will find attribution occurring' (Heider 1976: 18).

5: *Situations*. Attribution theorists have a pervasive tendency to attribute the causes of actions to situational requirements. 'Naïve scientists', of course, make the mistake of attributing intentionality where it is not, where the behaviour should probably be 'confined to its proper position as a local stimulus' (Heider 1958: 54). The 'fundamental attribution error' fixes on just such an issue. Some attribution theorists explicitly advocate situational explanations (Nisbett 1975), while for some the emphasis on the situation flows from a more deeply rooted adherence to behaviourist perspectives in which even the actor's activities are part of the situation (Bem 1972).

6: *Individualism*. The person is seen as responsible for evaluating and assigning causes. Heider's (1958) phenomenological sympathies and his emphasis on the role of intention in social interaction have been muted in later formulations on the theory by other writers. Positivist psychology prefers a more 'scientific' image of the person informed by natural sciences. However, the processes engaged in by the attributor are still conceived of as undertaken by an autonomous individual. So, 'The perceiver seeks to find sufficient reason why the person acted and why the act took on a particular form' (Jones and Davis 1965: 220). The various errors made by attribution theory's 'subjects' – their only potentially correctable misattributions – are, of course, individual errors. In addition, the sharp distinction between the 'person' and the 'situation' screens out attributions that might be made by a person to such things as social relations or shared knowledge.

Three paradoxes

As you will already have noticed, the assumptions which underlie attribution theory conflict with one another at a number of points. Certain contradictions stand out and the six aspects of the theory can be organized so as to form three pairs. Such a decomposition into binary oppositions is reminiscent of scientistic structuralist analysis. According to some structuralists, cultural forms and theories reflect universal polarities which govern human thought (Lévi-Strauss 1966). In this case we are simply using the device of pairing of assumptions into contradictory pairs as a convenient prerequisite for a *post*-structuralist analysis.

There is, first of all, an obvious conflict between the notions of truth and the appeal to relativism – between the supposition that misattributions can be corrected and the belief that attributions are not really right or wrong. Maybe attributions are relative, but for many researchers they are relatively *true*. They can only approximate an ideal, properly scientific, assignment of cause. In part, the status of real 'scientists' is at issue here. As Harré (1981a) points out, the experimenter chooses peculiar events so as to make the 'naïve' scientist's behaviour look odd. The ostensible relativism of the approach can then appear to be pretty feeble in relation to the power of the 'true' view. Attribution theorists turn their subjects into inferior versions of themselves.

Second, despite the much-vaunted turn to 'ordinary explanations' of social behaviour, attribution theorists only accept explanations which conform to their own notion of what is 'ordinary'. There is a conflict between the claims of science and those of common sense. The explanations given by ordinary people are deemed to be 'scientific' only after they have been carefully screened by the researcher. Attribution theory still carries out much of its research in the formal setting of the laboratory and is preoccupied with documents instead of the ambiguities of everyday speech. In this way an image of rationality is promoted, and only certain varieties of common sense are tolerated. We can only agree with the comment that 'Vestiges of the tradition of liberal rationalism, which sees science as fulfilling the role of demystifier still remain' (Billig 1982: 177).

Third, a conflict is conceptually produced between the individual and the situation. The split between individual and situational factors is maintained in the image of the person as seeker of causes. The individual is often expected to derive attributions from a situation of which her behaviour is but a component. These semi-behaviourist assumptions lead to a manipulative view of people and of the delusions individuals are prey to as they seek to understand their own actions as well as those of others. So, we are told, 'it is possible to induce a person to feel he [sic] has total freedom to express himself when in fact he has none' (Kelley 1967: 226). In some texts, the ability to 'situationalize' is seen as an ability of 'brighter' individuals. Here the contradiction between the personal and situational emphasis in the theory collapses into a wilful and cynical 'mystification'.

Ambivalence and ideology

There is an analysis of attribution theory which is sensitive to the power of ideology in social psychology. Michael Billig argues that the modern model of the coherent individual has broken down, and that nowadays 'the contradictions of contemporary capitalism might be reproduced, rather than concealed, on a psychological level' (1982: 203). In his view, ideology now comes to be reflected in cognition, and the ambivalence of attribution theorists towards, for example, the relation between the person and the situation, is one manifestation of the complexities of contemporary life.

Billig compares attribution theory with descriptions of the 'paradox of substance', where, in his words, 'Defining one phenomenon in terms of another involves the paradox of implying that it both resembles and ... differs from that other substance' (Billig 1982: 175). For example, in order to understand the activities of an individual, we need to specify the *situations* in which different actions can take place. The object of attention thus flips back to focus on its opposite. We can see such a conceptual switching from one extreme of each polarity which comprises attribution theory to the other: conceptions of truth are bounded by so many conditions that we eventually arrive at a form of relativism, and relativism must to some extent be 'true' to function as a theoretical position;

an examination of science will reveal it to be rooted in 'common sense', and our notions of common sense are modelled on standards set by science; and the person needs 'situations' as much as situations need the person to be understood as such.

A principle which informs this understanding of social psychological theory is that of rhetoric and the importance of conversation in the everyday maintenance of social relations (Billig 1987). These are notions which also lie at the heart of new social psychology, and we will return to them in Chapter six. For the moment it is possible to consider the discourse of attribution theory by taking account of its rhetorical character and moving beyond the types of paradox identified in Billig's work. The paradoxes which make up attribution theory are not merely ambivalently structured. One term in each pair is dominant. Once you realize this, we are halfway to a deconstruction of the theory.

Deconstructing attribution theory

The deconstruction of texts carried out by Derrida, which was described in Chapter three, begins by dismantling the conceptual frameworks which govern arguments. I will apply this now to the collection of texts – the discourse – which surrounds attribution theory, and show that the assumptions which inform a deconstruction give a special cutting edge when applied to this type of social-psychological theory. In deconstruction there is a thorough-going scepticism about the value of 'theory' as an alternative to the positions being unravelled; there is an emphasis on the intimate connection between 'intention' and context; and there is a rather pessimistic assessment of the possibility of escaping the logic which glues together the discourses in any culture. I will now take attribution theory through the three steps of deconstruction.

Three steps

The first step is to identify oppositions that are set up in the text. In this case we have the written discourse of the theory as a massive sprawling series of texts. The three key oppositions have already been described, but a deconstruction attends to the way the concepts are hierarchically structured. Consider the importance of truth and error compared with the meagre value that is placed on the accounts given by 'ordinary' people; the role accorded to the scientific status of research over the data sifted from naïve common sense; or the emphasis on the force of situations over unwitting individual actors. In all three cases one of the aspects is privileged over the other. The notions of relativism, common sense and personhood often appear as little more than rhetorical adjuncts (even though they are, at the same time, crucial to the internal structure of the theory).

The second step involves the displacement of the privileged term by its opposite number. A case can be made for the importance of the subordinate aspect of each pair. The terms can be turned around to reveal their opposites without too much effort, and it is evident that the subordinate aspects of the theory are *necessary* to those emphasized in the attribution theory texts. So, any notion of truth is contingent on some form of relativism because it is predicated on the particular nature of human beings (or of matter itself); science arose from, and is sustained by, intuitive commonsensical arguments; and a situation is defined as such by the presence of persons without whom it would not exist.

However, simply advocating one side against another does not escape the structure of the texts. We have to move on to the third step. This final step involves an attempt to transform the rhetoric from within by introducing a new term. I could elaborate a new meaning for an existing term and break the opposition down to prevent the dominant term from reasserting itself, and there are examples ready to hand from the discourse of new social psychology.

If we were to introduce Shotter's (1980) notion of 'joint action' into the first, truth/relativism, couplet, it might dissolve the separation of 'facts' from 'values' which is so crucial to positivist definitions of truth. Alternatively, the focus on 'self-presentation' advocated by Harré (1979) could highlight the power struggle involved in the final establishment of one view acknowledged to be 'true'. Again, turning to the second, science/common sense, pair, using the idea of 'joint action' would throw into question the dominant model of science which is predicated on the exclusion of common sense, and support instead a co-operative, interpretive style of human science. Stressing relativism, as Totman (1982) does, would also take away the force of the distinction between the ordinary and the scientific. Finally, in the case of the person/ situation dichotomy, an emphasis on relativism also draws attention to the way every personal, supposedly autonomous, action is defined by a situation and can only be understood within it. The idea of 'self-presentation' could be used to draw attention to the way individual actions are social *acts* for others and so require their presence.

I want to defer the problem of pursuing the third step of deconstruction until Part three of this book. In this chapter I want to focus on the problems posed by the ethogenic responses to attribution theory, and I will do this by looking at the way the *second* step of the deconstruction has been appearing in their discussions of the theory. However, a necessary preliminary to that task is a brief outline of the historical context of the theoretical debates and transformations I have outlined so far.

Cultural history

A curious thing about the three deconstructive paradoxes is that they come apart so easily. The tension between the polarities is obvious, and the case for the subdued aspect of each pair is relatively simple to make. In part, this is due to the impact of the debates which have surrounded the paradigm crisis. However, it also has much to do with the historical cultural changes, and the political and conceptual crises, which accompanied the conflicts inside social psychology. A deconstruction is not usually such a straightforward exercise, and a historical account would explain how the deconstruction of this particular theory was facilitated. The dismantling of texts always takes place in a context:

> The *incision* of deconstruction, which is not a voluntary decision
> ... does not take place just anywhere ... it can be made only
> according to lines of force and forces of rupture that are
> localizable in the discourse to be deconstructed. The *topical* and
> *technical* determination of the most necessary sites and operators
> – beginnings, holds, levers, etc. – in a given situation depends
> upon an historical analysis. (Derrida 1981: 52)

At this point, then, we should return to the analysis of systems of knowledge undertaken by Foucault. Foucault's (1970) descriptions of the forms of knowledge which governed the Classical Age which endured from around 1650 until 1800, and the Modern Age which followed it, will help us understand the significance of the deconstructive paradoxes which make up attribution theory.

The dominant form of knowledge in the Classical Age was a rationalist natural scientific method which led to human reality being seen as conditioned by natural causes. The notion of an autonomous 'self' or subject was not fully developed. The old paradigm in social psychology holds to just such a model of science and social interaction. Attribution theory, in like fashion, takes a rationalist view of behaviour. The concern with truth, science and the power of situations reflect the preoccupations of that historical period.

In the Modern Age, however, humanism rose in influence. An interest in alternative forms of human life developed. An anthropological conception of the variety of human experience arose, and with it a value was placed on personal 'truth'. The social world was generously assumed to be represented for each person as an individual reality, and the 'self' became seen as an experiential core of being, a subject which could be understood introspectively as the source of knowledge and action. We find such beliefs not only in new social psychology but also in attribution theory. Ordinary explanation and common sense are of value, truth is a matter for individuals, and individuals do the work of attributing causes.

A plausible conclusion would be that a deconstruction of attribution theory is possible because the inversion of conceptual priorities which it entails has already occurred in western culture, over a century and a half ago. In this case, social psychology lags badly behind mainstream culture. (This is yet another reminder of the isolation of the discipline from the real world.) A further consequence is that we should situate our own critical position in a historical context. This also applies to post-structuralism, to the development of deconstruction, and to the ability of a contemporary audience to appreciate the paradoxes of attribution theory. Here the argument that we are entering a postmodern cultural age is relevant. (I will discuss this claim in Part three.)

Attribution theory, then, carries with it the conceptual residues of two past historical periods. It is this which makes it so susceptible to a deconstruction of its main premises. What, though, of the ethogenic criticisms of the theory? I will now go on to address their arguments and show that the paradoxes which constitute attribution theory extend to its opponents. The deconstruction also needs to be taken into the new paradigm.

Deconstructing ethogenic responses

Some of the ideas developed in the various forms of new social psychology – 'joint action', 'self-presentation', 'relativism' – are useful antidotes to the presumptions of attribution theory. They could lead to the third step of a deconstruction. However, the specific responses by ethogenic writers to attribution theory have actually been limited to the second step of inversion, in which the subordinate concepts are championed. The problem is that the simple emphasis that the new social psychology gives to relativism, common sense, and individuality in its own texts leads it to repeat the three deconstructive paradoxes. Discussion of the inadequacies of ethogenic responses to attribution theory will also serve to demonstrate the importance of following through all three steps of a deconstruction. I will take, in turn, three of the responses to attribution theory from friends of new social psychology and relate each to one of the conceptual contradictions that have been identified so far.

Relativism substitutes for truth

This first response comes from a writer who is sympathetic to attribution theory and who attempts to reconcile social psychology's old and new paradigms. What happens if the relativity of accounts is taken seriously? Totman (1982) concentrated on this aspect of the theory, and argued that attribution theory reflects a shift to a 'relativist logic' in philosophy. Attribution theory does not, and should not, deal with 'truth' but with various accounts. This means that attempts to change an attribution might have the effect of 'disturbing cognitive structures which underpin perfectly adaptive lifestyles' (Totman 1982: 6). Totman goes on to make the claim that the problem of deception then disappears. Because all truths are relative, the notion of 'deception' no longer has any currency. The problem of deciding what is correct or incorrect dissolves, and with it questions as to who is right and who is wrong.

However, Totman does not allow this relativism to preclude any measure of the 'good'. There is an escape clause in his argument. The relativist logic of attribution theory for him is bounded by a powerful overarching truth. He proposes that the index by which the 'good' can be measured should be health, and this thesis underpins his earlier ethogenic study of health and illness in which the central dictum was that 'people, in their dealings with others, follow social rules. When they stop following rules, for whatever reason, they are likely to become ill' (Totman 1979: 20).

The relativism which is championed here, then, is short-lived, and we end up being sold an uncritical endorsement of the 'truth' about health which governs the dominant culture. The consequence is that the person as patient is disqualified from identifying deception because the powerful reply is that 'everything is relative'. In addition, the person cannot deceive the researcher because the objects of inquiry are not really accounts at all, but 'rules' which lie hidden within them. This means that research can carry on without a proper reflection on the moral order governing the situation and the surrounding society. Not only does this relativism presuppose a true standpoint from which social actors are liable to err, but processes of power and ideology are able to operate untouched. In this case, the relativism immediately invalidates the lay attributor's attempts to refuse to accept the definition of the situation laid down by the professional attribution researcher. This interpretation of attribution theory, then, deliberately sets up a power relation between people in which resistance is suppressed.

Common-sense substitutes for science

The next response comes from the mainstream ethogenic theory which has been most influenced by structuralism. What happens if the ordinary accounts are taken seriously? Harré (1981a) objects to the 'rhetoric of scientism' which, he claims, bedevils attribution theory. Attribution theorists such as Kelley (1967) are accused of projecting the model of rationality that scientists operate with on to the subjects they study. For Harré, the human being is a spontaneous creater of meaning, and ethogenic social psychology prioritizes common sense over the scientistic pretensions of traditional social psychologists: 'the conceptual systems of ordinary language must have priority over neologistic constructions and inventions' (Harré 1980: 211). A glaring problem with attribution theory, according to Harré, is that the researchers deal with written documents rather than with speech. Note here that the longstanding conceptual privilege given to speech over writing in western culture is reproduced in an ostensibly radical argument.

Harré links this bureaucratic theme in the research to the ethno-centric bias and rationalist ideology of American culture.

However, Harré's favour for ordinary explanation in ordinary language has its limits. There lingers a clear conception of what real rationality and science looks like, and he recognizes it in *speech*. Harré undertakes a contorted rhetorical manoeuvre to undermine the positivism of attribution theory which unfortun-ately (and predictably), in turn, draws ethogenics further into a rationalist model of human action: 'Our problem, as reformers, is to persuade Kelley that the people he has studied are rather like himself' (Harré 1981a: 141).

In this way the rationality of 'ordinary' people, those Harré calls 'folk', is uncritically appealed to. It is a rationality which must in turn correspond to Harré's model of rationality to be recognized by him to be pukka. The 'folk' must now display common-sense 'rationality' in order to be considered as genuinely 'ordinary' (just as their cognitive abilities and malfunctions had to be displayed to the attribution researchers). The result is that this common sense presupposes reason. Common sense which does not come up to that standard, even in speech, will be disqualified. Despite (and because of) the obvious humanist intent which informs this new social-psychological attempt to combat a bad theory, power and ideology are once again pushed into the background. We end up, then, with an ideological re-interpretation of an already deeply ideological theory in which conflicts over meaning are deliberately glossed over and resistance to dominant meanings is suppressed.

Individuality substitutes for situations

The third response comes from the most extreme phenomeno-logical position in new social psychology. Shotter (1981a) claims, in the course of his critique of attribution theory, that his herme-neutic standpoint is to the 'left' of Harré's. What happens if the individual agent is taken seriously as an author of actions? Shotter attempts to defend the individuality of the subject in the produc-tion of meaning. The fluid nature of accountable action is marked by an 'intrinsic intentionality'. This is then violated by attribution theory's model of the 'person-perceiver' as a searcher for 'causes' of actions. We do not attribute 'causes', Shotter says, but we do want to know how a person transforms 'the definition of the situation' in which they must act. An additional moral claim is that 'mental activity ... is *potentially* under one's control' (Shotter 1981b: 279). Attribution theory is understood as part of a historical process. He argues that it is part of a transition to a state of culture which suppresses real human intentionality 'with behaviour being explained by impersonal causes, and actions by reasons' (Shotter 1981b: 281).

However, although the person is 'autonomous', the 'author' of actions, she is governed by a drive 'to make their actions conform to something in their common sense' (Shotter 1981b: 279). This is a common sense which is shared. In addition, although action is carried out by agents, 'joint action' is accomplished by a person in coordination with others. Furthermore, it is only accountable with them. These assertions are advanced as part of an attack on empirical attribution studies, but they then fold ineluctably back into a situational position. People know what they are doing better than the attribution researcher, according to Shotter, but because of 'joint action' individuals 'are unaware of how its outcome is produced ... In such genuinely social activity, people may remain deeply ignorant as to what it is, really, they are doing (or why)' (Shotter 1981a: 177). The upshot is that the individual's agency is so limited that it is unlikely that they will, in practice, ever be able to exercise it completely.

It is worth recalling here the cynical attributionist argument that 'pragmatically' it would be better if individuals believed in situational attributions even if they were wrong. This position 'ends by countenancing mystification in order to produce better personalities' (Billig 1982: 182). Shotter seems to risk taking a correspondingly morally dubious stance when he argues that the fact of 'joint action' invalidates attribution research, but then supports the idea of human autonomy for moral/political reasons because without 'individually responsible and accountable elements, without in fact persons, a social order would fall apart' (Shotter 1981a: 174). Once again, although new social psychology attempts to oppose a dehumanizing theory, it finds itself caught up in the webs of power and ideology. In this case it fails to break from the assumptions which hold the theory together because it thinks it is more important to hold a social order in place than to support the resistance to it.

Repetition and opposition

The three ethogenic responses to attribution theory, then, each conclude with a repetition of the paradox they sought to overcome. Totman (1982), Harré (1981a), and Shotter (1981a) fail to break with the historically grounded assumptions lying within the theory. We have a telling example here of how new paradigm responses are unable to escape from the assumptions governing the old paradigm. The problem does not simply lie in the way ethogenics focuses on 'relativism' rather than 'truth', on 'ordinary accounts' at the cost of 'science', or on the 'individual' instead of 'situations'. The problem is that the *discourses* it draws upon in this culture invite it to describe social life or theory in such a way that it can easily fall into the grip of the commanding conceptual constructs. Furthermore, when social psychology, as an academic institution, brings in material from the 'ordinary' outside world it 're-frames' that material and so gives to it a different type of rationality. Social psychology cannot but give its own sense to the meanings it lets in.

Since Heider's first formulations of attribution theory various attempts have been made to give a sense to it that traditional social psychology would understand. There have been two trends. The first is sympathetic to the phenomenological side of the individual/ social divide. This trend invokes the memory of Icheiser (1949) who investigated the contents of the consciousness reproduced in 'collective representations' of the individual. Icheiser (rather dualistically) saw the 'data' of experience as 'the object of collective or the object of individual perceptions' (Icheiser 1949: 12). His observations have been advertised as providing some conceptual continuity between processes of attribution and the organization of those processes in shared 'social representation'.

The second reformulation has been in the dominant positivist tradition of social psychology which has downgraded individual agency in the service of scientific truth. Here, the making of attributions is seen as an individual cognitive activity. Some cognitions, including attributions, are about the encoding, storage and retrieval of social information, and so the term 'social cognition' is used. The whole reductionist paraphernalia of cognitive psychology is then used to explain social action (Fiske and Taylor 1984). This cognitivist terminology can then be used to co-ordinate the ostensibly more social 'attributional schemas' with others in the study of 'social representations'. That both a phenomenological-cal and a positivist route could lead to a study of 'social represen-tation' is not accidental, as I will explain in Chapter five.

As I have said, attribution theory is a relatively easy target for deconstruction. Its concern to produce a true account, using a scientific method operating on behaviourist principles which downplay individual agency in situations, is very much of a piece with the American tradition of social psychology. The individualist ideas were ostensibly relegated to the domain of sociology, but they lay buried within it, repressed and 'absent presences'. Here were the relativist ideas where pragmatism thrived, the good practical common sense which pragmatism sentimentalized, and the individualism of a burgeoning capitalist economic order which pragmatism celebrated.

Notwithstanding attempts to bring together the experimental and ethogenic paradigms in social psychology, new social psychol-ogists have been suspicious of attribution theory. As you have seen, though, it has been necessary to go beyond these suspicions and locate its contradictions in the matrix of the dominant culture. Because attribution theory was able to set the terms of the debate, new social psychologists were tied, from the start, to the guiding assumptions of the theory. Would the picture be different in the case of the theory of 'social representations' which emanates from Europe, which promises to draw upon sociological theory, and which new paradigm theorists have been *enthusiastic* about? This is the question that will be addressed when I turn to examine the theory of 'social representations' and the effects of the institutional divisions between the disciplines of psychology and sociology.

Chapter five

Social representations

The schism between psychology and sociology which made social psychology possible is full of paradoxes and contradictions. At first, the split appears simply to reproduce that gulf between the 'social' and the 'individual' which is such a powerful conceptual and experiential component of modern culture; sociology as a discipline uncovers the social facts and psychology reveals the laws of behaviour. If this were the case we would expect to find positivist (and then structuralist) methods reigning in sociology, and phenomenological (and hermeneutic) approaches dominating psychology. In fact the institutional cleavage between the two was not that simple. As with a broken mirror, the individual/social dualism which structured the relation between psychology and sociology can be seen within each fragment.

In the buffer zone between the disciplines where the social psychologies lie, the individual or social focus, ostensibly dominant in each of the two main disciplines, swing around to turn into their opposite. This is manifest in the peculiar way in which psychological social psychology focuses on the power of situations and adopts a behaviourist methodology in laboratory experiments, and sociological social psychology (the microsociology of Garfinkel, Goffman, and Mead) stresses the 'social construction of reality' (Berger and Luckmann 1971). When new social psychology imported ideas from microsociology, it failed to challenge deeply rooted assumptions about individual action and social structure, and ethogeny even reflected the rift between the two in its own texts (with Harré adopting a position sympathetic to structuralism, and Shotter defending hermeneutics).

The search continued for a properly social account of action which would leave room for meaning, and which would satisfy mainstream old paradigm social psychologists (who were always suspicious of the varieties of ethogenic solutions to the crisis). Now a theory has arrived from continental Europe which seems to fit the bill. 'Social representations' have caught the imagination of social psychologists in Britain – the battleground between European and American traditions and paradigms – and the theory promises to dislodge attribution theory from its grip on the discipline.

The problems and confusions in the social representations literature, however, flow from the same antagonisms which have bedevilled the study of social interaction since its inception. There is a struggle between the two disciplines. However, this has not stopped social-psychological mavericks in each discipline looking to the other in the mistaken hope that they will find what is lacking in their own. Sociologists look to psychology for an account of individual agency, and psychologists see sociology as the science of the societal backdrop against which their subjects behave. Supporters of social representations theory still mistakenly believe that solutions lie in sociology, and have been all the more desperate and uncritical in their plundering of orthodox sociological theory for ideas. This is a hopeless exercise, as you shall see. I will briefly outline the social representations position and what it borrows from sociology, and then show why it is so attractive to, and recuperable by, traditional social psychology. It will then be clearer why those who have studied social representations so far have been led to all but abandon the study of ideology and power.

'Social representations'

The 'theory' is, we are told, designed to be vague. The notion of social representations operates within a deliberately fuzzy framework, so that social psychologists can trawl for fruitful ideas without being constrained by overly scientistic criteria and definitions. The vagueness is also a result of the long incubation period between Moscovici's study of social representations of psychoanalysis in France in the 1950s, the suggestion that it may provide an alternative to traditional research into 'attitudes' in the 1960s, and the eventual 'first outline' of the theory to an English-speaking audience in the 1980s. A further contributory factor must be that during this time, Moscovici was, by turns, railing against American social psychology, rehearsing established denunciations of crowd behaviour, and conducting quite orthodox 'minority influence' laboratory experiments.

Social representations link images and concepts, and circulate in shared social worlds. In different situations, within different group settings, the social representations operate as 'the contemporary version of common sense' (Moscovici 1981a: 181). The study of these representations, Moscovici argues, amounts to 'the rediscovery of the social mind' (Moscovici 1982: 116). People employ social representations to explain social, natural, and mental phenomena to each other, and this shared 'reality' of images and concepts is nowadays constructed out of the stories told by modern science. As well as being useful communicative devices, social representations also serve to translate difficult formulaic principles into ordinary language. Moscovici also claims that social representations fulfil, in the process of this reformulation of science into 'common sense', a fundamental psychological need: *'The purpose of all representations is to make something familiar, or unfamiliarity itself, familiar'* (Moscovici 1984: 24).

You should start to get suspicious about the theory when we learn that the world of social representations emerges out of an individual psychological motivation common to all cultures, a 'genuinely universal principle' (Moscovici 1982: 124). It operates as a point of resistance to the panoply of strange and alienating bureaucratic ideas which threaten contemporary creative thought. There are, Moscovici says, two worlds of meaning, or universes, in our society.

Consensuality

Social representations comprise the 'community of meanings' which form the consensual universe. It is here that we feel 'at home, sheltered' (Moscovici 1981a: 189). A social psychology which explored the social representations of this consensual universe would have to be one which respected and valued this 'common sense'. Attempts to discover the social representations of a culture or subculture would also require some sympathetic understanding of the forms of thought found in the system of signs which holds the world together as a meaningful place. Here the programme of research Moscovici suggests links with the proposals made by new social psychologists during the paradigm crisis. Past ethogenic studies could even, at a pinch, be reinterpreted as examples of 'social representation' research (Harré 1985).

The elicitation of social representations, then, is more than just a methodological perspective. The project also rests on a moral critique of modern society, and a decision to support, reinforce and reproduce the consensual universe. Social psychologists who chose this option are recreating a sort of psychic breathing space which permits the full flowering of personality and conversation. Moscovici goes so far as to offer Paris cafés as examples of sites of this 'conversation'. In such genuine 'conversation', we are told, 'Thinking is done out loud. It becomes a noisy, public activity which satisfies the need for communication' (Moscovici 1984: 21). Although Moscovici gloomily notes that 'the art of conversation' is vanishing, we are consoled with the thought that the ('universal') processes of 'familiarization' and 'communication' which produced social representations will repeatedly revivify it.

Reification

There is the second universe of meanings, however, which continually intrudes into the consensual system. In the reified world things appear as isolated objects. People existing in such a world are cogs in a bureaucratic machine, and have to conform to already given roles and categories. The reified universe contains the system of decontextualized 'facts' which make up 'Science'. (Modern scientific ideas must be translated into the consensual universe because they are not expressed in the terminology of the 'ordinary language' which lay people understand.)

According to Moscovici (1982), we are moving into an 'era of representations', but, at the same time, the bureaucratization of the 'social mind' continues apace as reification grows with the power of scientific ideas. In the reified world, 'The social body depends on a sort of global environment and not on reciprocal agreements . . . science is the mode of knowledge corresponding to the reified universes' (Moscovici 1981a: 187). If we look to mechanistic science as a solution, therefore, we break knowledge down into self-contained, task-specific routines, and so threaten genuine 'communication'. One consequence of this position for social psychology is that Moscovici pre-empts discussions of fact and value. He signals the immediate moral correlates of choices of research strategies and topics. Either we collect 'facts' and 'data' and stand guilty of reinforcing reification, or we pursue 'values' and 'meanings' and sustain consensus.

Structure and meaning

Time and again in Moscovici's papers on social representations, concepts occur which reproduce the Saussurean semiological (and later structuralist) proposals for a science which would study the 'life of signs' in societies. A 'social representation', for example, comprises an 'image' and a 'concept'. Moscovici (1984) attempts to bridge the gap between the internal, subjective world, where concepts lie, and the external outer 'reality', where images can be found. The connection between the 'image' and the 'concept' is, he says, the same as the relationship between two sides of the same piece of paper. Saussure (1974) made just such an analogy when he talked of the link between 'signifiers' (the 'sound images') and 'signifieds' (the 'concepts'). The 'signs' then become the medium for what we understand to be 'communication'.

Unlike structuralists and post-structuralists, however, Moscovici does not follow through the implications of what this new notion of 'communication' must be like. The study of signs should involve a radical transformation of notions of meaning, seeing meaning as located *between* persons in language and interaction rather than within each of them. An 'idea' of 'concept' or 'meaning' is not folded into a word and then sent to another person to be unwrapped and so 'understood'. A word and other collections of signs have a meaning by virtue of social context and the other signs which are present (or significantly absent). This is why the decoding of items from a text or discourse can proceed without the presence of the 'subject' acting as an authority for the 'true' meaning.

Moscovici's problem is that he holds to a received (traditionally hermeneutic) modern view of meaning to safeguard the distinction between consensuality and reification. The person engaged in a genuine 'conversation' is busy creating thoughts and communicating them to another mind through the channel of social representations.

Along with judgements as to what constitutes 'genuine' communication go traditional distinctions between 'true' individual thoughts and 'distorted' social processes. Not far behind follows the distinction between a proper spoken conversation and mediated, written documents. Here is a manifestation of 'the dominance of an entire metaphysics of proximity, of simple and immediate presence' (Derrida 1978: 130). Moscovici implies that the closer ideas seem to the individual mind (for example, in conversational speech), the 'truer' they are. Post-structuralism responds to this line of argument by connecting the sentimental view of meaning, and trust in 'communication' that attends it, with the forms of philosophy and human science which dominate western thought.

Structuralism as such does not, of course, hold all the answers, and the contradictions and problems in that approach, as with the solutions offered by post-structuralists (such as Derrida), have to be worked through to be made useful. However, were Moscovici to have placed the study of social representations in *that* theoretical frame, he could have avoided some crucial problems. As it is, the debt that Moscovici does acknowledge is to the traditional schools of sociology (Durkheim explicitly, and then, hidden inside, as a necessary complement, the work of Weber). This is a debt traditional social psychology is only too anxious to honour, for the interest still remains with the sovereign individual.

Sociological representations

The term 'social representation' adapts Durkheim's (1953) distinction between 'collective representations' and 'individual representations' to the needs of social psychology. The aim is to occupy a 'strategic middle ground' between the two levels of analysis (Farr 1981: 251). The problem is that the definitions Durkheim gave for the two varieties of representation were intended to ensure that a conceptual space be left open for psychologists to fill. He insisted that the laws which organized societal systems were theoretically separate from the laws governing the activities of the individual mind. The conceptual space Durkheim left open – a place for the *individual* to act – is present in almost every sociological theory.

In this sense, Durkheim's work reflects the internal structure of the discipline of sociology. Within sociology other traditions, less happy with positivist psychology and surer of the value of method-ological individualism, seize that space. Weber is one of the mainstream sociologists who does this. Consequently, the import-ation of sociological theory into social psychology, through the theory of social representations, also brings with it the social/individual dualism which informs the debates between the Durk-heimian and Weberian schools.

Structure

Durkheim insisted that although the individual mind was a micro-cosm of the societal *conscience collective* and reflected it, the mentality of groups was not the same as that of individuals. Within the 'collective representations' comprising them are 'social facts' which operate externally to the individual. These work, Durkheim asserted, 'independent of his [sic] individual will . . . endowed with a power of coercion, by reason of which they control him' (Durkheim 1938: 2–3). They weigh down on the mind of the person as objective things, and for this reason are amenable to 'scientific', positivist study. Organic imagery is often used to describe the relationship between the two levels of analysis: 'individual minds in relation to the cerebral cell and social facts in relation to individuals' (Durkheim 1953).

As well as being a positivist Durkheim was a determined functionalist. In practice, his sociology was consonant with a conservative position. His ideas exemplified traditional sociology's function in the investigation and protection of social structures. Not only are 'individual representations' separate constructs, but the picture of the ideal–typical scientific observer that Durkheim constructs is of a rational individual. Individuals, then, must be able to separate from the social world. In the practice as well as in the theory of Durkheim's work, one level of the research enter-prise (the study of 'collective representations') mirrors the other (the study and experience of 'individual representations').

Phenomena

Individual experience and action are the focal points of Weber's sociology. The latent, and necessary, individualism in Durkheim's work is given expression and attention in Weber, and the two writers enjoy a more or less peaceful coexistence in the discipline. For Weber, the individual actor plans action in accordance with her interpretations of the possible actions of others. Action is social 'by virtue of the subjective meaning attached to it by the acting individual' (Weber 1968: 258).

The social action Weber champions, however, is under threat. He was concerned that changes in the organization of society affected the degree to which it could be realized. Against human agency stood the growth of the bureaucratization of experience, 'reification' as the impoverishment of spiritual life: 'The fate of our times is characterized by rationalization and intellectualization and, above all, by the "disenchantment of the world"' (Weber 1967: 34). Here, Weber is concerned to resist the very processes that Durkheim considers to be necessary and valuable. Durkheim saw the lawfully organized social world as a legitimate object of study, and thought that awareness of society's 'collective representations' amounted to a progressive 'hyperspirituality' (Durkheim 1953: 130). Weber, on the other hand, resisted the encroachments of this bureaucratic system of 'social facts' upon individual agency. It is this 'agency' that Moscovici optimistically champions (Parker 1987b).

Psychology's sociologies

A further twist occurs when sociological theory is represented in social-psychological texts. Within sociology, the Durkheim and Weberian traditions are both complementary and mutually exclusive (though there were attempts to botch the two together in American sociology). The research carried out on either side, and the debates as to the merits of each, spread into thousands of journal papers and books. When social psychologists draw the ideas across the disciplinary boundaries, simple characterizations are given of each position and there is a pretence that one coherent position can be distilled from the two. On top of that, this imaginary position is laced into the prevailing cultural constructs outside the academic world. At the moment, those constructs are still thoroughly individualistic.

The licence for individualism is already present in Moscovici's recent suggestions as to how the crisis in social psychology could be remedied. We should, he says, engage in '*the anthropology of the modern world*' (Moscovici 1981b: viii), and give it 'a phenomenology rather than an epistemology' (ibid.: x). For social psychologists this advice is only too easily read as an invitation to continue the incorporation of sociology into their work and take Weber on board alongside Durkheim. In the edited volume in which the 'first outline' of the theory of social representations appears, for example, the editorial gloss sets up a distinction between 'simple behaviour' and 'meaningful action'. A number of 'classic theorists' are cited – Wundt, James, Mead, Durkheim, Weber – as all purportedly demonstrating that 'internal representations and information strategies' have a 'social nature' (Forgas 1981: vii). This is not simply a squashing together of incompatible ideas. This 'representation' of the theories also has the function of legitimating an existing laboratory-experimental paradigm of research in social psychology (buttressed by attribution theory) which now goes about its business under the name of 'social cognition'.

Mainstream sociological theory is being read in such a way as to sanction the absorption of social representations into the burgeoning literature of 'social cognition'. This reading and re-writing of the theory is accomplished in two interrelated steps. The first flows from the assumption that a more humanistic understanding of the individual than that implied in Durkheim's writings can be produced by turning to Weber. The second step involves the attempt to study this human agent as if it contained the 'representations' Durkheim claimed existed at the level of society. A consequence is that whether social representations are supposed to be equivalent to 'collective representations', whether they are seen as a mediating variable between 'collective representations' and 'individual representations', or whether they are supposed to dissolve the distinction between the two, becomes irrelevant. Because the 'representations' are imagined to operate inside the individual's head they are, effectively, '*individual*'. So, for all the talk about finding a more 'social' inter-disciplinary social psychology, Durkheim's original prescriptions for a division of labour between sociology and psychology are followed, and social/individual dualism is reinforced.

Social paradigms

Moscovici claims to have produced a theory that has at last broken out of social psychology's hopeless 'archipelago of lonely paradigms' (Moscovici 1985: 91). Unfortunately, the project of social representations cannot but be written within the terms of debate in a discipline still resonating with the crisis and the clash between old and new paradigms. Each side is ready to assess and select new material to shore up its own position. On the one hand, the laboratory-experimental tradition has recovered ground with the success of attribution theory; on the other, the ethogenic opposition is anxious to grasp fresh ammunition to escape from its still marginal position. The old tradition has started to recuperate Moscovici's ideas within the field of 'social cognition' (Parker 1987b).

'Social' cognition

Once the individual 'subject' has been conceptually re-created in the space left open by Durkheimian positivist sociology, and reinforced by Weberian phenomenological accounts, the way ahead is clear for social psychologists to fill it with cognitions. Writers in the old paradigm rationalize this individualism with claims that the cognitions are 'about' social things. 'Social cognition' in American social psychology deals with processes of encoding, storage, and retrieval of social information. It looks at how the individual employs schemata which make the world intelligible and predictable. Attribution theory is concerned with one aspect of this process. Already social representations are being absorbed into social cognition research. The 'first outline' in English of the theory of social representations appeared in a volume entitled *Social Cognition: Perspectives on Everyday Understanding* (Forgas 1981). This, of course, was a title designed to appeal to attributionists attracted to 'lay explanation'. (Already in British developmental psychology, individualistic stories of cognitive development and linguistic skills are being told to account for supposed sequences in the acquisition of social representations.)

The retreat into cognitivism means that we now have all the disadvantages of methodological individualism (positivism and reductionism) without any of the advantages. Again, some of Moscovici's own statements warrant this retreat, and the fault lies not simply in the vagueness of the theory which permits different interpretations, but in the inconsistency, and even occasional mischaracterization, of the research. For example, in practice, the research on social representations in France has, in the vast majority of cases, involved content analysis of interviews, papers, television, and other mass media (Farr and Moscovici 1984). What is described in the literature is the *content* of shared expressive realities. In this there are similarities with the material produced in Britain by ethogenists.

However, at some points Moscovici leads us to believe that a preoccupation with the content of social knowledge is being replaced, in social representations research, with a focus on *form*. This would involve an invitation to 'social' psychologists to discover general rules for the processing of information. Moscovici argues this in a revealing passage: 'the content of thinking and talking matters less than formal aspects of thought and language. This distinguishes the study of social representations from the study of schemas, attributions and the like' (Moscovici 1985: 91). Although he attempts to set some distance between his own position and cognitivism, the contrast he sets up will not cut any ice with cognitivists.

Moscovici's claim also collapses the European opposition to American social psychology (which he was once responsible for firing) into a tame proposal for a different perspective. In the wake of Paris 1968, he depicted American social psychology as infected by individualist ideology. Now he suggests that work on social representations is a European approach to 'social cognition' 'different from, and complementary to, recent North American research' (Moscovici 1982: 182). In line with the logic of this position some of the French researchers have already returned to the laboratory to introduce 'representations' into the minds of 'subjects' and then observe changes in behaviour (Farr 1984).

'Social' meanings

Moscovici's proposals restate some of the tenets of the ethogenic arguments put forward during the paradigm crisis. Moscovici does, at some points, attempt to block a return to positivism and individualism. He argues that thought is public, and explicitly opposing 'the implication of any clear-cut division between the outside world and the inner world of the individual' (Moscovici 1973: xi); here he is in accord with the most radical of Harré's (1983) and Shotter's (1984) attacks on dualism in social psychology.

Some of the tensions I have mentioned within the social representations literature have been noted and accounted for in different ways by other writers sympathetic to the European tradition.

One response comes from mainstream ethogenics (Harré 1985). According to this analysis, the key distinction which we must be aware of is that between social knowledge as a 'collective' plurality and social knowledge as a 'distributive' plurality. New social psychology contends that social meaning is collective; it is shared in such a way that the rules in any social world are not all present in one head. Each person contributes to the material in the expressive sphere, and their imperfect knowledge becomes cogent when it is co-ordinated with the knowledge of others through acting and accounting. The collective plurality of social representations, then, could be discovered by gathering material from many informants. Such studies on notions of health and illness, for example, have been translated already (Herzlich 1973). Often, however, the research slides into necessitating a 'distributive' view, with each item assumed to be contained in every person. The experimental studies rest on just such an assumption (Farr 1984). The problem with the distinction between these two types of plurality is that it implies that we could faithfully adhere to a 'collective' sense, share our knowledge with a researcher, and then forget about *how* knowledge is distributed. It is not possible to wish away conflicts of meaning and the way some accounts are continually *repressed*. To pretend that it is looks uncomfortably like pluralism (the position that everyone's voice is valid and heard), and would not take us any further towards an understanding of ideology or power.

A second response is advanced by advocates of 'discourse analysis' who recognize the difficulties Moscovici tangles himself in when he assumes that there is 'consensus' of social meaning (Potter and Wetherell 1987). However, for these discourse analysts, notions of power and ideology are not yet built into their approach. They *could* be added later, after an analysis of discourse has been carried out, but there is no reason why different discourses should not be described as if they were just bits of language. For the new discourse analysts, following in the wake of new social psychology, the term 'discourse' covers 'all forms of spoken interaction, formal or informal, and written texts of all kinds' (Potter and Wetherell 1987: 6). There is no necessary sense of organization, structure or system. When themes are identified, the term 'interpretive repertoires' is used, and we are given the impression that these could just as easily be the possession of individuals as of the collective. The definition of discourse Potter and Wetherell offer is more acceptable to social psychologists, and very different from the definition Foucault gave, in which discourses are 'practices that systematically form the objects of which they speak' (Foucault 1972: 49). I have followed this post-structuralist view more closely when I have argued that we should see discourse as collections of texts, as *sets* of statements which construct objects.

Social changes

One important respect in which Moscovici has gone beyond most social psychology has been where he has given the theory an historical character. His statements about the cultural changes which have accompanied the emergence of social representations as a field of study raise questions about the status of the whole discipline of social psychology. He claims that we are moving into a 'new era of representations' (1982), and that although culture has become increasingly divided into consensual and reified universes, we can take solace in the way that social representations act as a point of resistance and the way in which the study of them is warranted by shifts in other cultural and academic areas. We can take particular comfort from the progressive movement in psychology, away from positivism, which he links with changes in art; he claims that 'Just as painting has returned from abstract art to representational art, psychology has reverted from behaviour to consciousness' (Moscovici 1982: 117).

However, although Moscovici draws attention to cultural changes, he does not go far enough. He does not escape from the terms of debate which constitute modern social psychology – the dualism which permits both an abstraction of the key items of 'data' from their context and their representation in a mechanistic account, and which rests on the division between behaviour and consciousness. We have, in Moscovici's statement, a clear expression of deep-rooted conceptual structures which tie him to *modern* social psychology (Parker 1989). To step beyond those dualities, I have to return to a theme touched on earlier in the chapter, and place the social representations literature in the context of structuralist and post-structuralist ideas. It will then be possible to move on from the paradigm crisis terms of the debates to take up the repercussions of the conceptual and political crises on social representations social psychology.

Representation, structure, and struggle

The use Moscovici makes of sociology, and the particular reservations, caveats, and additions that are given in the representations of Durkheim in the social representations literature, are paralleled in the other human sciences in the debates over the benefits or otherwise of structuralism. Both Durkheim and Saussure share a conception of society as a social reality, and it is hardly surprising that structuralist anthropology (Lévi-Strauss 1966) and political theory (Althusser 1971) received a sympathetic hearing when their texts entered sociology.

The new work on social representations strengthens the influence of structuralism in social psychology. Now Durkheimian theory is representing, again, a structuralist way of investigating forms of social interaction in smaller social worlds. Unfortunately, social psychology has not learnt the lesson that the result is a positivist approach to meaning which conceals within it a phenomenological individualism, and that we are receiving across the massive gulf between psychology and sociology, much in the manner of light-waves from a distant planet, a method that has all but burnt out in its place of origin. Furthermore, the structuralist attempts to build a theory of ideology failed in much the same way as the social representations research has. Just as structuralism came to be seen as a problem rather than a solution in philosophy and literature, so it is with the theory of social representations in social psychology.

Concepts of ideology as a 'thing'

The problem lies, in large part, with the use of the term 'representation'. For Moscovici, what is represented derives from social 'reality': 'there is nothing in representation that is not in reality, except the representation itself' (Moscovici 1982: 141). One

103

'representation', then, is a representation of a complete stock of knowledge contained in a society, and a particular way of picturing and evaluating an individual person's knowledge of their social world is reinforced. We are led to speculate how far, and how imperfectly, an external system of meaning is reflected in internal cognitions.

A political consequence is that even if social representations are not seen as 'deposited in the brain of each individual' (Saussure 1974: 23) as semiology argued, it appears that the key to enlightenment is that they *should* be. This, presumably, would then facilitate perfect 'consensual' transparent 'communication' between people. You should recall that Moscovici's appeal during the paradigm crisis of the early 1970s was for social psychology to study all that pertains to ideology and 'communication'. In his theory of social representations, the two concepts are still twins but have now become *counterposed* so that the latter ('communication') is thought to be the point of resistance and the solution to the power of the former ('ideology').

In literary theory the development of structuralism rested on just such a counterposition. Through the 'scientific' study of underlying structures, it was proposed that the 'competence' of readers could be increased so that they could appreciate more of the meaning of the text (Eagleton 1983). A version of this is also found in new social psychology, in equations between 'ideal cognitive resources of individuals' and 'coupled with known deficits', 'the actual resources of real individuals' (Harré 1979: 185). This latches into crude mechanistic notions of 'false consciousness' in ideology, which suppose that it emanates from distorted cognitions: perhaps certain individuals merely lack access to the main 'accounting systems' of a society (Harré 1977: 332). This is a reductionist account of ideology with an individualist solution.

When Moscovici does talk of ideology, it is as if it were a type of 'thing' which could be identified (and so dispelled). He claims that social representations act as a sort of intermediary stage in the process of the diffusion of scientific knowledge across a culture. After the 'scientific' phase and the 'representative' phase come the 'ideological' phase, when thoughts are 'appropriated by a party, a school of thought or an organ of state' (Moscovici 1984: 58). Again, there are uncanny echoes of structuralism, this time of its expression in political theory. Although Moscovici (1984) alludes to (caricatured Althusserean) structuralist political themes when he complains about theories of ideology which picture people as dupes, he barely acknowledges his own debt to these ideas. it would be as well for readers to be aware, not only of Althusser's (1971) contention that ideology is 'a system of mass representations' embodied in certain powerful institutions (the Family, the Church, and Education), but also of the realization by his erstwhile supporters that his view implies that there were real things outside the representations which can show whether they were 'true' or 'false'. It was a reaction against the notion that there was anything 'outside the text' that led disillusioned structuralists to turn to Foucault's (1977) account of discipline. Foucault usefully showed that traditional notions of ideology as a 'thing' presupposed a 'truth', and that his descriptions of 'regimes of truth' more effectively emphasized the power of meaning, of discourse, to *create* the things we think are real. The problem is that he led many radicals to drop the term 'ideology' altogether, and this has had disastrous political effects outside social psychology.

Concepts of ideology as a relation

The alternative that post-structuralism was led to adopt was to describe the meandering of meaning, not in terms of 'representation', but in terms of *signification* (Henriques *et al.* 1984). This is more useful for three reasons. First, the notion of signification allows for the fluidity of meaning and takes account of the way our understanding of terms changes from context to context depending on our social positions. This feeds into a view of ideology as a *relation* instead of a thing, with different meanings enabling or disempowering different writers, readers, speakers, and listeners. Second, because it allows for the idea that our talk in texts and discourses creates the social-psychological phenomena that appear to be innocently 'discovered'. Discourses and texts give a 'reality' to the objects delineated within them, and so the circulation of such discourses has immediate effects of repositioning people who 'read' them. The discourses position people, and social-psychological discourses always position their 'subjects' without power.

The third reason for adopting the notion of signification is that it cuts across the dualism which nourishes the space for the 'individual' (and for an academic discipline like social psychology which continually reduces social issues to that level of analysis). I want to retain the distinction between the practical order of society and the expressive order, and not fall into an extreme relativist position. Studies of geography, biology, demography, and economics can reveal the *practical* possibilities for, and limits to, human action. This does not mean that the stuff of social psychology does not have a 'real' basis outside of the expressive sphere. The notion of signification here follows post-structuralism in refusing to aim the metaphor of 'depth' at individuals, resisting the siren calls of 'social cognition', so skirting the Scylla of positivism (and structuralism) and the Charybdis of phenomenology (of hermeneutics). We should take care to resist the temptation to think that nothing 'outside the text' affects what happens within it, or that there are *only* 'regimes of truth'. It is crucial that the term 'ideology' be retained, not for what it refers to (for it does not, anyway, refer to a 'thing'), but for what it *does*. To use the term 'ideology' to talk of systems of meaning which screen out conflict and repress resistance is to connect with radical politics outside social psychology, and to *empower* people.

The politics of power

Were we to deconstruct the theory of social representations we might take the consensual/reified distinction, and show how the ideal of consensus threatens always to become 'reified'. The very social representations which give expression to our thoughts are but reconstructions of scientific thought. They come about through processes of 'anchoring' and 'objectification' to ameliorate our 'instinctive dread' of powers beyond us, and they 'intervene in our creative activity' (Moscovici 1984: 7). Moscovici then paradoxically calls for a 'science' of social representations to beat back reification. The science of the consensual then starts to seem suspiciously similar to the scientism of the 'reified' universe. This move is similar to that outside social psychology when scientific structuralism would end up reproducing 'a world of calculable and representable subjectivity' (Derrida 1982: 317). Laboratory-experimental social psychology plays the same game when it attempts to measure and explain away experience and social meaning.

The danger is that the other organic images of the social to be found in Durkheim's writings would also come trooping back. The notion of the social 'body', for example, holds within it notions of deviance and pathology which necessitate those modes of policing Foucault (1977) discusses in his writings on the rise of disciplinary power. The programmes to subject the 'social body' to certain treatment regimes then fold back on to the individuals contained within it. Individuals are invited to take care of processes of 'self'-discipline. Foucault's (1981) account of the emergence of confessing subjects in modern society indicates that calls for a return to an idealized 'genuine' communication against reified worlds could *intensify* the powerlessness of people. The acceptance of certain discourses – feeling 'at home' in them – makes for the success of a regime of 'truth'. There have been many previous attempts to dispel 'ideology' by producing a 'calculable subjectivity', among them those of the original *idéologues* after the French Revolution, which accompanied the birth of modernity (Billig 1982).

To drag across material from mainstream sociology to solve crises in psychology, as with the theory of social representations, does not dissolve the barriers between the two disciplines. Neither does it challenge the experiential chasm between the 'social' and the 'individual'. The ground plan of the academic disciplines is laid out in such a way as to vitiate attempts to solve the crisis in any one of them by borrowing from the others. This is the case with structuralism and when I turn to attempts to span individual intention and social meaning in the next chapter you will see that it could even be the case with recent appropriations of post-structuralist theories of the text.

Chapter six

Conversation

Neither the turn to lay explanation which was filtered through rationalist American social psychology, nor the attempt to raid sociology made by European social psychologists in order to develop an account of social representations, has succeeded in resolving the problems thrown up by the paradigm crisis. However, some sort of interdisciplinary work has to be generated to provide an alternative to the easy option of remaining fixed in the old terms of the debate. This chapter is concerned with the nearest social psychology has got to taking seriously the developments in post-structuralism. Some writers in the ethnomethodological strand of sociological social psychology (microsociology) have started to take advantage of the similarities between their own writings and those around deconstruction, mainly in literary theory. Ethnomethodology has been drawn on by new social psychologists, and recently has served as an important resource to those concerned with discourse theory (Potter and Wetherell 1987).

Readings

Two purposes can be served by looking at the recent readings of deconstruction in microsociology. The first is that we can draw some lessons about the uses we can make of deconstruction. We will see once again how tempting it is to absorb a different system of thought into existing categories. Descriptions of ideology and conflict are excluded in the process of translating Derrida's work into the microsociological discourse. The second purpose is that it emphasizes the importance of drawing on *other* writings in post-structuralism and informing our reading of Derrida with the historical perspective given by Foucault (1977, 1981) on power and resistance. We will then be in a position to understand the dangers of appealing uncritically to the notion of 'conversation', and taking the 'self' as given.

Conversation

Conversation is becoming more popular in the human sciences, and many unwitting participants are being roped in. Both Hegel and Wittgenstein, we are told, shared the view that the activity of philosophy was that of a conversation (Lamb 1979). Heidegger and Dewey are brought together to support the programme for a 'post-philosophy' which would continue the conversation (Rorty 1982). Even behaviourists have jumped on the bandwagon and suggested that Skinner could join in (Lamal 1983). In social psychology, we have already heard Moscovici's plea that we should return to conversation as the exemplary form of a consensual universe. New social psychology has long advocated that good ordinary language could dissolve the neologisms which abound in the discipline: 'the fundamental human reality is a conversation' (Harré 1983: 20).

Images of circles of friends communicating in conversations, and by that activity alone dissolving ideology and power, are appealing. If we could just keep talking and not panic, perhaps the social problems and culturally constructed divisions between us would disappear, or maybe they would be shut out of our little social worlds, 'moral communities' designed to survive the 'new dark ages' (MacIntyre 1981). However, not only are these images idealistic, they are also dangerously sentimental. This rhetoric which appeals to the notion of conversation *appears* to dissolve power relations but actually dissolves attempts to take those relations seriously.

Conversation does seem to be one of the most fundamental of human realities, and this idea is connected with the fact that it is a spoken form of interaction. It has a place in the conceptual infrastructure of western discourse as a more immediate, genuine form of communication than bureaucratic, dehumanizing, written documents. We should take care though, for here is another manifestation of the speech/writing hierarchy, one of the metaphysical oppositions deconstructed in Chapter three. An alternative concept adopted in this book which subverts this hierarchy, and which blocks the return to individualistic notions of 'intention' which lie at its heart, is that of the text.

Text

Our problem now is that deconstructive descriptions of the text are being drawn into an unhappy alliance with traditional notions of the conversation. Ethnomethodologists are coming across Derrida's writings and using them in sociology. Derrida's (1978) deconstruction of structuralism, which spearheaded the development of post-structuralism, is itself being reconstructed by ethnomethodologists who have taken up his ideas. The descriptions he purportedly provides of a continual escape of meaning from individual intention can be used to conjure up a social world in which an infinite variety of meanings is possible. Ethnomethodology, which has long been under attack for its pluralism and evasion of coercion in sociology, seems to draw on Derrida less as a topic than as a resource. Out of this blend of ideas has emerged what I term 'textual sociology', a strain of work which is in turn being borrowed by the new discourse theories in psychological social psychology (Potter and Wetherell 1987).

The characterization of deconstruction which this textual sociology promulgates – as encouraging a 'free play' of meaning and interpretation – does not, however, accord with that given in Derrida's own texts. In literary theory, where deconstruction has found the most active readership in America and Britain, there have been attempts to bring out the implications of the approach for an understanding of the social construction of power and subjectivity (Eagleton 1983). There are the resources available for us to produce an account of the forces operating on interpretations of ideological texts, and the power of the institutional frames which contain the discourses which inform texts.

The main task of this chapter, then, is to prevent the notion of conversation from assimilating that of the text, and to insist that, to the contrary, our conversations are structured by texts and the power relations contained within the surrounding discourses. I will briefly outline the contribution of ethnomethodology, describe the convergences with deconstruction which have led to the development of textual sociologies, consider some of the misreadings of

Derrida, and then follow some more useful routes through literary theory.

Sociality and textuality

Within microsociology and literary theory there is a new, thorough-going scepticism. Ethnomethodology and deconstruction put in question the verities of their own disciplines, and, in the process, unsettle received paradigms.

Ethnomethodology

Ethnomethodology stakes a claim for small-scale social interaction. The focus is on everyday procedures people use to make sense and order in the social world – their *ethno*methodologies (Garfinkel 1967). Notwithstanding its roots in traditional positivist American sociology, phenomenology has had a major influence, and when there is any structure to action, it is seen as the accomplishment of social actors. Ethnomethodology offers a critique of orthodox sociology which it sees as engaging in a particular construction of rationality. This sociological rationality explains away the creative activities of the subjects it studies. Sociology's interpretations are not of something 'outside' but are of other interpretations or-ganized within a chosen (or an implicit) theoretical frame. Socio-logy imagines that its use of theory enables it to strip away the 'glosses' (presentational artefacts) at work in members' accounts, not realizing that what it finds underneath is simply a construct in its own explanation of social life.

Ethnomethodology turns to the practical sociological reasoning produced by society members. The ever-increasing number of interpretations layered upon interpretations in everyday life are the means by which life is rendered rational (rationally account-able). It is a mystification of this activity to degrade the importance of this common-sense accomplishment in favour of sociological categories such as 'class' or 'society'. In the accounts are the procedures that give a reality and solidity to social life. These are the rituals which make up 'a common sense knowledge of social structures' (Garfinkel 1967: vii). The study of the methodology people employ to bring about and reproduce this common-sense knowledge involves the elucidation of 'formal properties', but

111

these properties are understood as in process, '"from within" actual settings, as ongoing accomplishments of those settings. The formal properties obtain their guarantees from no other source, and in no other way' (Garfinkel 1967: viii).

What Garfinkel calls 'the artful practices of everyday life' (Garfinkel 1967: viii) are the only bedrock for research, and these practices reproduce the reasoning produced in the 'indexical' expressions of the social actors. The notion of 'indexicality' is used to remind microsociologists that the terms used in members' accounts are bound to context. The meaning and force of an item of speech or of an episode can only be understood in its relation to the surrounding social world. The fact that expressions are irremediably indexical also undermines traditional sociology's attempt to gain an 'objective' understanding of what is going on. Sociological expressions which masquerade as 'objective' explanations are revealed to be so many instances of objectification, or reification, the treating of social accomplishments as if they had a reality separate from members' meanings. Ethnomethodology thus parts company with Durkheimian recommendations that 'social facts' should be treated as if they were things. At the same time it laments the inevitable process by which members appear to forget the indexicality of their products.

The social nature of meaning robs expression of any original purity the moment it finds itself in the world. Experiences are not the property of an individual, but can only be known through *others*. So language, which is in the domain of others, enables the actions of a person to be experienced, but language also simultaneously blocks any immediate contact with the reality or 'truth' of action. A consequence is that actions continually undergo a process of 'typification', and 'The accounting process is automatically or, as Garfinkel says, "essentially" reflexive upon the experiences themselves, depriving them of their uniqueness and specificity at the very moment, and by the very process, that they become known at all' (Filmer 1972: 213). While ethnomethodology attempts to trace the networks of practical reasoning which weave this first-order objectification, the crime of traditional sociology is that it accomplishes, within its own reasoning, the raising of objectification to a higher, 'second-order'.

Garfinkel's challenge to sociology has therefore entailed a shift in microsociology's understanding of the development of knowledge and of individual experience. Ethnomethodology's refusal to root the practices it studies in the cognitions of individual members, or to take those cognitions as the source of social life, has facilitated a convergence with writings in post-structuralist philosophy and literary theory. Attempts to centre the creation of sense in the cognitions of speakers, listeners, writers, or readers are rebutted in Derrida's deconstructions. Garfinkel's writings are also important because his radical objections to sociological reasoning apply just as much, of course, to social psychology, where new social psychologists have used them to good effect (Shotter 1984). However, the textual sociologists are only willing to follow this process part of the way.

Convergences with deconstruction

There are a number of points of contact between ethnomethodology and deconstruction. It will be sufficient, for the moment, to identify three of them.

1: *Methodology*. How is it possible to uncover the rules, the common-sense network of presuppositions, that comprise social life? The technique of 'garfinkeling' is one attempt to make present the unspoken assumptions of interaction by breaking down rituals from within. The tacit becomes seen as necessary, and its pattern is thrown into relief when people try to reconstruct it. The self-conscious repairs of the order disrupted by the 'garfinkeling' ethnomethodologist allow the researcher to see how that order works. So ethnomethodology, having recognized the dangers of attempting to construct a theoretical frame around the theories of those it studies, works inside social life, disrupting and forcing clarification by the social actors themselves. Just as ethnomethodology works from within the social rules, so deconstruction insinuates itself into the terms of the text it interrogates. Deconstruction is also sensitive to the way overarching theoretical constructs can unwittingly reproduce what they had hoped to overthrow. Deconstruction breaks apart the architecture of the text, 'using against the edifice the instruments or stones available in the house' (Derrida 1982: 135).

2: *The social construction of meaning*. Indexicality of expression involves the wedding of meaning to language and to the context in which it is employed. The 'glossing' (interpretive) practices of speech make the person giving the interpretations part of *shared*, and fluid, 'intentions'. This puts into question the notion of the individual as cause, and it becomes impossible to turn to events inside the head of an actor for the explanation of action. Instead of being a property of the individual, for example, 'motives' are taken to be public and collective. What orthodox sociology and psychology take as a cause is redefined as an effect, and this in turn effects the social construction of selves: 'For any member to ascribe a motive is thus to do no less than to generate a person' (Blum and McHugh 1971: 108). This move is effectively a deconstruction of causality which calls the old Cartesian opposition inside/outside into question. The 'outside' is not reinstated as the final cause, but the relationship between the two terms is overturned. Ethnomethodology and deconstruction are thus subverting appeals to an inner essence, whether it is defined cognitively (mechanistically) or phenomenologically (experientially).

3: *Errors*. An extreme form of the forgetting of indexicality and the misattribution of origins of meaning is found in academic sociology. An example is the labelling of 'deviance', of the 'errors' of others. The trap is that ethnomethodologists are often led to imply that the 'ordinary practical reasoner' is always pathologically deviant. 'Labelling' risks being seen itself as a pathology. It is difficult for ethnomethodology to conceive of cultural circumstances in which the reification contained in rational discourse may be absent. A similar gloom pervades Derrida's work. For all the liberation of meaning deconstruction seems to promote, the lures of metaphysical discourse are ever present. Deconstruction finds itself engaged in perpetual house-cleaning. In the case of 'madness' as a form of deviance, for example, Derrida argues (against Foucault's romantic descriptions of unreason before the advent of modernity) that all discourse presupposes 'normality' and an 'other', the unreasonable thought outside. Deconstruction and ethnomethodology share the thankless task of exposing the forms of error that govern discourse, and neither can pretend ever to offer a final escape route.

Some ethnomethodologists have sighted a sister soul in deconstruction, and so far there have been two aspects to the desired communion of the two. There is, first of all, a series of attempts to use Derrida's work as ammunition against orthodox sociology. This is a paradoxical exercise in theoretical buttressing, because both deconstructive and ethnomethodological approaches eschew theory. It is, though, precisely the common antipathy to any overarching 'metaphysics' (in deconstructive jargon) or 'program-matizing' (in ethno-speak) that attracts each to the other. The other aspect of the attraction is the increasing importance accorded to language in the human sciences in general, a phenomenon attributable to the influence of structuralism in different dis-ciplines. The varieties of ethnomethodology which draw on lit-erary theory have been given an extra boost by the development of post-structuralism (and the more mechanistic structuralist method has continued in the conversation analytic studies which do purport to discover formal properties of speech).

Textual sociology

The turn to language, and the interest in deconstruction, has produced a new blend of critical work. This emerging textual sociology will now, as it grows, form a powerful pole of attraction for psychological social psychologists (Potter and Wetherell 1987). This is all the more reason why we must ask whether the burgeoning textual sociology can cope with the old, justified, sociological criticisms levelled against ethnomethodology. There are problems relating to power and ideology that are still avoided. It is useful to recall the argument advanced in *The Coming Crisis of Western Sociology* (Gouldner 1972) that ethnomethodology lacks any conception of the world as structured in favour of certain interests, and that it gives instead a sense of life as 'a diffuse multiformity of values rather than a clearly-structured conflict of political and ideological groups' (Goulder 1972: 391). There have been changes in the surrounding political and academic climate. While the 'almost Nietzschean hostility to conceptualization and abstraction' (ibid.) was raised once as a charge to damn ethno-methodology, now Derrida's declared debt to Nietzsche gives the textual sociologists a defiant confidence in their position.

However radical and outrageous the first burst of ethnomethod-ology in sociology had been, the complaints in that discipline's 'crisis' literature were never adequately answered. A major failure has been that the supposed 'decentering' of the individual as an imagined unitary 'self' was not completely accomplished. There was a loss of nerve at the prospect of a thoroughly constructionist view of subjectivity, and the individualism sociologists claim to avoid was, as ever, protected. This is the individualism that lies at the heart of textual sociology's keeping with conversations instead of tackling texts.

One of the advantages of new social psychology was that it opened up further the questions which had been raised about the historical specificity of social-psychological phenomena (Gergen 1973) and gave accounts of the 'self' as culturally-produced (Heelas and Lock 1981). In Harré's (1983) writings there is an emphasis on the way that language (organized in the 'primary structure') allows individual responsibility to come into being in different ways in different societies. Post-structuralism takes this account even further. Derrida (1976) shows how subjectivity is produced not outside, but within texts. Foucault (1981) explores the notion of individual subjectivity as an historical construction bound up with discourse and with power. I want to emphasize this constructionist view of individuality, and the way it must be linked with an account of power and ideology. The activities of the textual sociologists provide an object lesson on how to *evade* these most radical aspects of post-structuralism by appealing uncritically to individualism. They do this in their accounts of the roles of speakers and listeners in conversation.

Speakers and listeners

I will mark three points on the road to the new literary-theoretical pole of microsociology. The studies which fall at those points will serve to illustrate the limit to the 'decentering' of the individual that has taken place. To varying degrees, the three positions retain a confidence in the 'self' and its ability to reflect upon, to produce, and to control meaning. Although the movement of language in 'texts' is taken into account, the assumption remains that underneath the constraints of language there is, finally, individual expression. The 'subject' as speaker or as listener is guaranteed its meaningful place. I have selected texts by Coulter (1979), Liberman (1982), and Silverman and Torode (1980) because the three operate as conceptual reference points for my narrative.

'Conceptual phenomenology'

Coulter (1979) does not directly encounter literary theory. His work, however, has been influenced by the 'linguistic turn' in philosophy, and his translation of psychological attributes back into the social domain echoes deconstruction's suspicion of essentialism. He shows that our experiences of our 'selves' 'are constituted for us by intersubjectively-shared reasoning procedures and modalities of situated language use' (Coulter 1979: 34). Thought is seen as mapped within ordinary language rather than being viewed (as in most cognitive psychology and social cognition research) as having 'the same ontological status as an object hidden in a box' (Coulter 1979: 14). Emotion is described as resting in a network of 'affect-concepts', and varieties of emotion are depicted as being dependent on 'specific arrays of meaningful circumstances' (Coulter 1979: 127).

However, the process of giving meaning lies at the core of Coulter's understanding of intentionality. This leads to his failure to understand the coercive aspects of language. According to Coulter, language as a shared net of meaning does not *necessarily* distort individual expression. There is, rather, 'a kind of solidarity built into the orderly functioning of talk' (Coulter 1979: 22). Although power may enter, although 'asymmetries' could occur, the intelligibility of communication ensures that these are exceptional circumstances. Coulter is led to advance a position which rests on the plurality and goodwill of language (and the good wills of those within it). This leads to a cosy view of human interaction, and it folds comfortably into the concept of symmetrical 'conversation' as a haven from coercion. Coulter successfully describes the organization of different realities in discourse and the way appropriate mental predicates are reconstructed in talk, but the operation of power is an issue that is foreclosed: he says 'There are no such things as social "forces" triggering or coercing cognitions – only social procedures (which may or may not be followed) and culturally-conventional orientations (which may be violated or ignored)' (Coulter 1979: 156).

'Semiotic sociolinguistics'

With Liberman (1982) we move a little closer to deconstruction and a little further from the intentions of speakers. Liberman

117

moves beyond phenomenology to hermeneutics and hopes to radicalize it by explicitly combining Garfinkel and Derrida. The project for a semiotic sociolinguistics, then, also takes us into the realm of 'social texts', and the expressive work of the speaker is always reciprocated by the creative work of a listener.

Not surprisingly, the picture Liberman constructs is close to Garfinkel's own formulations. The spoken word immediately becomes a 'public facticity' and so 'the orator's speech is his thought' (Liberman 1982: 307). Understanding is described as dependent on the reflexivity of members' accounts. Liberman's paper does take up some of the shared concerns of ethnomethodologists and post-structuralists. One of these is the suspicion of metaphors of 'depth'. Liberman quotes Garfinkel as commenting that 'There is nothing behind the looks of things – things are what they appear to be' (Liberman 1982: 307), which is a sentiment central to post-structuralist literary theory: 'there is nothing beneath: the space of writing is to be ranged over, not pierced' (Barthes 1977: 147).

However, Liberman's characterization of his approach as being hermeneutic is unfortunately all too accurate, and it is here that he breaks with deconstruction. Language is not meaningful because it can be interpreted to uncover deeper truths but because it is a *text*. Liberman falls back to the assertions in traditional hermeneutics that underneath meaning there is a basic level of pre-linguistic sense. He rather sentimentally contrasts 'open', 'global', 'non-autonomous' Australian Aboriginal expression with 'restrictive', 'linear', 'autonomous' English. Not only does he romanticize Aboriginal expression, the biggest problem in English, he says, is that the *listener* risks being 'stripped of part of his [sic] communicative role' (Liberman 1982: 302)

Liberman here reproduces the move that Lévi-Strauss made in structuralist anthropology when he blamed writing for threatening the authenticity of speech. As Derrida (1976) pointed out, this judgement appeals to a conception of 'the natural' as a 'presence' which guarantees 'true' meaning. The rhetorical appeal to 'the natural' occurs not only in biologistic forms in psychology and sociology, but can reappear in critical texts when they appeal to natural states of conversation. Liberman, then, partially deconstructs the role of the individual speaker in controlling meaning, but passes part of the task of commanding meaning over to the individual listener. 'Conversation' is presented (as in Moscovici's work) as an ideal which the reified world of the West has almost suffocated, but which speakers and listeners together can keep alive.

'Interruption'

Finally we move on to the third and ostensibly most radical attempt in microsociology to dislodge the individual from the centre of the social world. Silverman and Torode (1980) range over a number of theories of language, and while the general framework stems from Garfinkel, it is Derrida who is acknowledged as the direct inspiration for their study. They argue that the notion of 'interpretation' itself presupposes a reality underneath social meaning, and that it should be replaced by the term 'interruption'. Garfinkel's interruptions then provide models for 'powerful ways of transforming the everyday world' (Silverman and Torode 1980: xii). They refuse to set up any hierarchy of texts and would, for example, be supportive of deconstructive objections to Liberman's differentiation between creative and restrictive conversation.

Nevertheless, they endeavour to champion the authenticity of *all* everyday language, and this returns them to precisely that aspect of ethnomethodology which denies the force of constraints, of power relations: 'the reality is a play of speeches, referring to each other in contradictory ways which permit no speech dominance over others' (Silverman and Torode 1980: 135). Furthermore, in the pluralistic 'play' of speeches are the possibilities for 'interruption' by *listeners* (who then become speakers). This means that although they have refused to speculate about the nature of 'Being' or ontology (preferring to stick to the 'ethno-ontology' of the 'folk'), they still save space for an individual who is free to 'interrupt'.

This idealized listener, and the activity of interruption, are predicated on the supposed 'free play' of the text which allows unlimited room for manoeuvre. A pluralistic reading of Derrida is presented, then, and while the intentions of the speaker might have been deconstructed more radically than in Coulter's (1979) and Liberman's (1982) texts, the price Silverman and Torode pay is to assume that all restraints could be lifted from the persons weaving within it. They are the last of the reference points on the roads to deconstruction, but we are left with a pluralism that pretends that *anyone* may interrupt the text.

As textual sociology develops, then, the absolute freedom of the text is assumed to enable the listener's as well as the speaker's role to blossom. Coulter supposes that there is a symmetry between speakers and listeners resting in the solidarity of talk: Liberman protects the meaning-giving role of the listener in creative speech; and Silverman and Torode create the listener who interrupts and overturns at will the speaker's position. While the self-conscious activity of the individual who produces texts has been questioned, they have yielded to the temptation to replace it with the individual who consumes. All the while this dissolves the value of deconstruction in the service of an idealized notion of communication and conversation. If we turn to the uses of deconstruction in literary theory, however, we will see conceptions of coercion in the texts that contribute to conversations.

Writers and readers

Within literary theory, the consequences of deconstruction have included a demotion of the texts ordinarily deemed to be properly 'literary', and it has become necessary to explain how the canon of literature came to be demarcated from 'lesser' writing (Eagleton 1983). This has led to a concern with the way the institutions which frame the texts also coerce writers and readers within them. Literary theorists who have used Derrida's post-structuralist work have also had to deal with the switch of emphasis from the writer to the reader in high structuralism, and the way that all the while the notion of a final 'authority' for true meanings remained. I will briefly sketch out the debates that parallel textual sociology's shift from speakers to listeners before defending Derrida.

Literary texts

The first wave of structuralism involved, in a famous phrase, the 'death of the author' (Barthes 1977). The codes of literature were seen as being reproduced regardless of the intentions of the person who committed them to paper. The meaning of a text, then, could not be explained by reference to the wishes and thoughts of the

120

individual whose signature appeared at the end. Instead, structuralist analysis promised to transform literature into a scientific discipline which would unearth the underlying laws. Far from defeating dualism, though, this opened up a dichotomy between author-based and reader-based criticism. Because the intentions of the writer as author had been ruled out of court, a *reader*-based analysis came into its own.

Not only could the literary 'scientist' imitate what she presumed to be done in other sciences, but the positivist division between 'facts' and 'values' was also reproduced. The analysis could be handed on to other readers so that they too could gain insight into the text. The genius of the author was replaced as the touchstone of truth with an ideal competence or mastery of the reader. A 'correct' reading of texts was thought to be possible, and so a careful schooling was required to initiate an aspiring reader into the necessary techniques. Some advocates of structuralism attempted to open up the codes of the text to competent readers.

The shift to post-structuralism and deconstruction involved a critique of such a scientist search for 'structure' that fixes the meaning of a text and 'dreams of deciphering a truth or an origin which escapes play in the order of the sign' (Derrida 1978: 292). This did not automatically solve all the problems of course, and even some of the outlines of deconstruction have set up dichotomies between 'theory' and 'practice' which look to the ingenuity of the individual user as the most important determinant of its success: 'The truth is that deconstructionist theory can only be as useful and enlightening as the mind that puts it to work' (Norris 1982). As in microsociology, the adoption of a 'correct' approach does not guarantee that it will not be understood 'incorrectly'.

What the textual sociologies extract from the debates in literary theory is the notion of indeterminacy of expression and plurality of meaning. If this were right, the individual would be left with the freedom to interpret (or interrupt) whenever and whatever she liked. Deconstruction is depicted as allowing for this when it resists attempts to place truth in structures or in persons and instead 'affirms play' (Derrida 1978: 292). It does look like a warrant for the extreme subjectivist strand of sociology, and Derrida's opponents claim that he paints a relativistic picture of perpetual and unrestricted interpretation.

Coercive texts

Despite Derrida's detractors, there are forces in the text that deconstruction takes into account. Three points about the deconstructive view of coercion in texts should serve to show why texts cannot be thought of as components of the power-free conversations idealized of late in microsociology and social psychology.

First, there are issues to do with *power*. When post-structuralism insists that *'there is nothing outside of the text'* (Derrida 1976: 158), this has the function of ensuring that interpretations cannot proceed with an external referent, model, or 'transcendental signified' which is apart from texts. All that we understand about the world is, by virtue of that understanding, endowed with meaning. It is, in some way, part of a text. However, this does not mean that what lies beyond the text does not affect what can be said. What is 'pre-text' insinuates itself in the contours of the text. The practical order affects the way power is distributed in the expressive realm of society. Take the example of Derrida's discussion of Lévi-Strauss's idealization of the time long ago before 'writing' poisoned 'speech'. Central to Lévi-Strauss's case is a romanticized picture of the Nambikwara people before writing arrived, and 'the nature of the organism submitted to the aggression of writing' (Derrida 1976: 119). Derrida makes the point that far from this being a good and happy time, it was a strictly hierarchical society with relationships 'marked with a spectacular violence' (Derrida 1976: 135).

The deconstruction of the speech/writing hierarchy proceeds (as described in Chapter three) by positing a 'writing', or *text* which includes speech, so saying that all society necessitates some kind of 'writing'. The correlate of this is that no society exists without some kind of violence. The two-fold consequence of this is that Derrida does not deny the existence of extra-linguistic coercion: 'military or economic violence is', he says, 'in structural solidarity with "linguistic" violence' (Derrida 1976: 135). The violence then gathers a particular quality when it becomes embedded in the shared worlds of meaning that texts (spoken or written) make possible: 'writing cannot be thought outside the horizon of intersubjective violence' (Derrida 1976: 127).

The second point is to do with the question of *ideology*. Within the text the notion of *'différance'* (Derrida's neologism for the way items differ from one another and defer a final meaning) involves conflict. This *différance* is characterized as an active 'discord of . . . different forces and of the differences between forces' (Derrida 1973: 149). The much-advertised 'free play' of meaning does not necessarily licence an endless and infinite variety of interpretations ready to be plucked out from any text. There is no fixed meaning in the text (as structuralists claimed), yet the shifts in meaning are determined. The relationship between the reader and the text, and the constellation of texts available at any particular time, result in an intertextual matrix which constrains and constructs what can be produced. The different intertextual matrices which hold human society together are termed 'discourses' in this book. Derrida quite rightly denies that he is a pluralist, and does argue for a 'hierarchy' of plausible interpretations. In a deconstruction, 'meaning is determined by a system of forces which is not personal . . . the field of different forces, the conflict of forces . . . produce interpretations' (Derrida 1980: 21).

It is therefore a mistake to think that deconstruction sanctions the individualist shift from writers to free interpretations 'based only on the fantasies of the reader' (Derrida 1980: 22) (or from speakers to the free activities of listeners). Some interpretations are more plausible and powerful than others, and the deconstructive approach must be part of a theoretical understanding of the work of texts, whether they be literary texts or texts in spoken conversation. In addition, this means that the theory/practice distinction dissolves. Deconstructions are not formulated first and then 'applied' afterwards: 'Deconstruction is not *neutral*. It *intervenes* (Derrida 1981: 93).

The third and last point about coercion in texts is to do with the relationship between deconstruction and history. Some writers in literary theory have made connections between the activities of writing and reading and the economic structures of society (Eagleton 1983). The deconstruction of conceptual structures depends on historical circumstances (as we saw in the deconstruction of attribution theory in Chapter four). The 'conflict of forces' permits certain interpretations and reveals certain conceptual hierarchies in texts and discourses. The political thrust of deconstruction, then, is toward a critical social theory which would have as its aim the subversion of constraints rather than a simple redescription that would leave things as they are.

Institutions

The historical dimension is highlighted when deconstructions connect with the intersection of different texts found in institutions. The important function of institutions in the interpretation of texts has recently come to the fore in literary theory, with Derrida being cited as an ally in the process of deconstructing them. Derrida argues, for example, that 'It is by touching solid structures, "material" institutions, and not merely discourse or significant representations, that deconstruction distinguishes itself from analysis or "criticism"' (cited in Weber 1982: 60). These institutions come into being at certain moments in history, produce certain texts to buttress them, and then resist attempts to dismantle them to make way for something better.

The question of the institution as a frame for readings (with the term 'frame' holding pictorial and criminal connotations) is also broached by deconstruction. What is normally taken to be an external limit enters into what it encloses. The frame works to affect everything that lies within it. Once again the conceptual stakes are that the hierarchy inside/outside is taken apart and what deconstruction unravels are the texts which support varieties of essentialism. The political stakes are that institutional struggles are constituted by external relations between them and other institutions.

The structuralist attempt to fix meaning in a text or a behaviour (as in experimental social psychology), or phenomenological attempts to fix meaning in individuals or accounting subjects (as in new social psychology) is not just an academic issue. The activity of deconstruction has a political relevance. Fixing meaning in the writer or reader or in the speaker or listener always involves some degree of coercion. Microsociologists attempting to recuperate deconstruction refuse to recognize this, and so they find the notion of 'conversation' appealing. They ignore a key lesson from deconstructive literary theory in their selective readings of the literature: 'To establish or institute a state of mind, a particular interpretation can only involve an exercise of force, even violence, in order to arrest the inherent tendency of signs to refer to other signs, *ad infinitum*' (Weber 1982: 62). My proposals at the end of Chapter eight are designed to help radicals break out of the 'state of mind' which holds the institution of social psychology together.

Social psychology has, since it was constituted in America in the early years of this century, at the temporal centre of the Modern Age, been trapped in the same institutional vice which grips all individuals in this culture. Inside academic social psychology, those radicals who appeal to the 'ordinary', 'consensual', or 'everyday' world are trapped between the categories provided by psychology or sociology. Even in the textual sociologies, texts reproduce images of individuals *separated* from social relations. These are power relations which determine the types of resistance that can be developed. Social-psychological texts are not innocent 'misrepresentations' of social action. They nourish the discourses outside the discipline which construct objects (such as 'attributions', 'prejudices', or 'emotions'). They reproduce models of people who are only rational and trustworthy when alone, and become irrational and dangerous when they engage in collective action, and it is here that social psychology as an *ideology* works. It is here that conflict in society is covered over or 'resolved', and that we see ideology as the combined effects of power relations in discourses and texts.

I have struck a critical distance from social psychology in Parts one and two of this book, and this has involved a historical analysis and critical distance from modern culture. This has been possible because within society there are always spaces for resistance. In recent years there have been suggestions by poststructuralists (and others influenced by them) that modern culture is finally breaking down. Even texts in social psychology (those influenced by the textual sociologies) have been celebrated as the heralds of *postmodernity*. This description of culture can provide a critical vantage point for the conceptual issues arising from the paradigm crisis in social psychology. Whether or not this is sufficient and whether the notion is a useful point of resistance for *political* issues, are matters that I will now turn to in Part three.

Part three

Alternatives

Now we are in a position to understand that the crisis in the discipline was part of wider cultural changes. I want to show in these last two chapters that radical work in social psychology has to be pursued both in the sphere of culture outside the discipline where the stuff of social psychology is dreamed into being *and* in the institutions inside where social psychology is formalized and practised.

Chapter seven is concerned with culture, and in particular with the transformations in social interaction and self-understanding which have attended the emergence of postmodernity. First I will consider what a *postmodern* social psychology might look like by piecing together the descriptions of social action that our culture now encourages. We should tread carefully though. The implications of uncritically adopting postmodern culture as the template for a new approach would be pretty grim.

One useful contribution made by new social psychology is its distinction between the expressive sphere, where meanings are circulated, and the practical sphere where the physical necessities of life are answered. I want, despite the arguments of uncritical enthusiasts for post-structuralism and postmodernity, to hold fast to this distinction. But I shall modify it, pour my own meanings into it. The material I will deal with in Chapter seven lies in the expressive sphere of social life, and in this sphere the 'realist' hopes of the mainstream ethogenics inspired by structuralism (in Harré's work) will always come to grief. Realism will not work when applied to discourses, and texts. In the expressive sphere, where cultural and historical meanings lie, the thoroughgoing scepticism of post-structuralism is useful. The problem is that this scepticism can be given an unhelpful political twist when it turns its gaze to the *practical* order of society. It can lead to an apolitical or liberal relativism which cannot accept the reality of conflict and resistance.

In the practical order, which new social psychology deliberately chooses to neglect, on the other hand, a realist account *can* be given. Economic, climatic, demographic and biological factors do yield up to a scientific observer regularities of 'cause' and pattern. It is in this practical sphere that post-structuralism has little purchase. This does not mean that the modes of investigation of, and meanings attributed to, this practical sphere do not change as the expressive order changes. It does mean that a political account of the phenomenon of social psychology must be based on an appreciation of issues other than those normally addressed by social psychology itself. At this point we must take social psychology as an *institution* seriously. The split between psychology and sociology not only prevents social psychology from understanding the nature of ideology and power, but that split makes it unlikely that it will ever be able to generate useful knowledge about those phenomena.

In Chapter eight I turn to the way the institution of social psychology has built upon practical divisions of labour in the 'real' world. As I move back inside social psychology, therefore, I consider the various political positions social psychologists have proposed to solve the crisis. What is the crisis other than a real contradiction – the appearance of conflicting discourses in a text? Such a crisis should be pushed by radical social psychologists as far as it will go. One way of organizing the various solutions that have been put forward is to map them on to the modern and postmodern positions I discuss in Chapter seven. This is useful but not good enough, for debates over the nature of modernity and postmodernity alone could obscure an account of the ideology and power which glue social psychology together. Can we save social psychology by gradually improving its methods and building better theories, or should we reject the whole enterprise as a dead end, a diversion from a properly progressive understanding of social relations? By considering these questions you will at least see how the conceptual responses to the crisis in the discipline have political repercussions, and then be able to take some steps to end it.

Chapter seven

Culture

Modern social psychology draws upon modern culture for theories and descriptions of social action, and critiques of the discipline must also extend beyond the boundaries of the discipline. Some approaches in social psychology, and almost all of those which fall within the old laboratory-experimental paradigm, fit so comfortably within the old dominant culture that it would be a vain and pointless endeavour to try to prise them free of it.

The identity between the discipline and its society raises the question of whether we could escape modern social psychology by using material from the emergent *postmodern* culture. This would, after all, be a logical step given that the post-structuralist ideas I have considered in Parts one and two of this book are effectively an expression inside literary theory and philosophy of the postmodern age which encloses them. In this chapter I will draw upon some of these ideas to sketch out what a postmodern 'social psychology' might look like.

The picture I paint, however, will not be reassuring to those of us who have been seeking to give an account of ideology and power in social life. The purpose of my extrapolation of postmodern tendencies will be to raise an alarm, and to urge caution. What is 'popular' as the dominant cultural form of any age is not necessarily *progressive*. We should adopt a more critical stance toward postmodernity, to accentuate its positive progressive features and avoid its reactionary implications.

Postmodernity and language

The idea that a changing language can recategorize a changing world to the point of recreating it is well known to students of the media. From the moment the behaviourist J. B. Watson fled for Madison Avenue and the psychoanalyst A. A. Brill advised advertisers on how to encourage women to smoke, warnings have been sent to the unwitting public about the activities of 'the hidden persuaders' or, nearly half a century later at the cusp of postmodernity, how we need to 'decode advertisements'. Those working on the analysis of popular culture, for example, draw attention to *The Hoover Book of Home Management* which invites us to identify three types of dirt; these categories have the deliberate effect of provoking us to buy the different appliances for each variety (Williamson 1987). For social psychologists, on the other hand, the notion of language producing concepts is brushed under the carpet as just another residue of Sapir-Whorf. The institutions of psychology and social psychology lag behind the expressive sphere of the 'real' world and the ideological transformations which affect it (as well as the structure of the practical order which underpins those transformations).

What is emerging in postmodern culture outside social psychology is an awareness that language can construct different realities, that discourses can construct objects. While social psychologists are still using the behaviourist terminology of social facilitation theory to describe the subjects they observe in lavatories, other vocabularies can be developed in the outside world. If the name of a village in the north of England is plucked out of an atlas, say, alternative meanings can be poured into it which will more appropriately capture a new experience: 'Kettleness (adj.). The quality of not being able to pee while being watched' (Adams and Lloyd 1983: 80). Such a definition makes no pretence to be universal or final. It carries with it a sense of being local and provisional, and draws attention to the 'reality' it conjures into being. ('Middlemist (vb.). To equivocate unsuccessfully when asked for an explanation of scientific activity in public loos.')

Each of the metanarratives which were thought to organize the modern world and propel us toward enlightenment has broken down to the extent that, so the new story goes, we inhabitants of postmodernity have even lost our nostalgia for the lost narratives. As the social construction of human attributes is made salient, all 'real' positions disappear. Even rhetorical devices are seen only as *fictions*. We know, for example, that there is no sarcasm on Betelgeuse (Adams 1977: 15). The turn to language as the creator of meaning, and the turn away from anything other than language as a source of explanation, has accomplished two things. It has, at one and the same time, given a new twist both to old American pragmatism and to new ethogenic critiques of the positivist behaviour fetish which transfixed social psychology for its first fifty years.

The deconstruction of each of the three aspects of the Classical Age of reason and the Modern Age now finds its end in language: the relativism, which displaced beliefs in absolute truth, is twisted further under a post-structuralist emphasis on discourse and texts as the grounds of reason; the common sense, which displaced science, is also seen as organized into the language games in which science is an equal partner in the search for pragmatic usefulness, and the 'self' loses its position as the central creator of meaning as its dependence on others becomes seen to be constructed by language. Postmodernity provokes an attitude of uncertainty, of studied doubt, and any attempt to gain knowledge involves a continual reflexivity which underlines the provisional and transitory nature of that knowledge. This doubt and reflexivity also informs and subverts self-knowledge. Postmodernity is *différance* writ large. A corollary of this is that it becomes implausible to hold apart the categories of philosophy, epistemology, and ontology. I will follow its effects in the areas of representation, action, and investigation and work down through the layers of culture that press in on our understanding of social psychology.

Representation

The idea of postmodernity originates in discussions of changes in architectural practice. One influential account of the end of modernism in architecture names the date, and the time: a high-rise modern housing block in St Louis was pulled down in 1972 at 2.32 in the afternoon, and with it the great reform projects to construct total environments (epitomized in Le Corbusier's desire to construct the house as a 'living machine') came crashing to the ground (Jencks 1977). Now architecture is increasingly promoted as being 'multivalent' and 'multicoded', with frivolous snatches from the past often pasted on to pastiches of high-tech design. Gothic columns started to appear on car factory sheds, Japanese pagodas on school playgrounds, and egg cups on breakfast television studios. Postmodern architecture draws attention to itself, and to its own construction, through these devices, and so it is that heating, electric, and air conditioning entrails have sprouted from Paris arts centres and London banks.

Out of architecture came postmodern languages for classical music (Philip Glass), pop (Laurie Anderson) and postpunk (Half Man Half Biscuit), as well as cinema(*True Stories*), theatre (Berkoff), and dance (Merce Cunningham). Just as architecture displayed itself as 'post' (a popular shorthand term which competes on the continent with 'pomo'), so the different varieties of postmodern culture have sold themselves by drawing attention to their own artificiality, and generated a massive parasitic literature on those forms as representatives of postmodernity. References to post-modernism are even to be found in free British Rail magazines (Pawley 1987). The obsession with self-reference, and a commentary on the 'unreal' status of the art forms, then feeds into everyday descriptive vocabularies for things as 'real' or 'natural' as emotions. Eco (1986) points out what while a modern expression of affection might be 'I love you madly', the postmodern rendering might be 'as Barbara Cartland would say, I love you madly'. Even before devotees of deconstruction could get their hands on it, the notion of 'love' itself slips away from the realms of 'pure' meaning and intention, into culturally constructed webs of signification.

American soaps have long revelled in this postmodern self-referentiality, with pretences to 'represent' the real world mocked through devices ranging from Pam in *Dallas* dreaming a countless number of past episodes so the scriptwriters can wipe the slate clean, to celebrities appearing in *Dynasty* as 'themselves'. In traditional British stodgy BBC soaps, the subversion of modern representations of settings and characters has been slower, but no less dramatic. Take *The Archers*, which started as 'an everyday story of country folk' in 1950, broadcast eleven times a week on Radio Four. The fictional village of Ambridge started to produce faked newspapers and autobiographies as early as the 1960s, but by 1987 the game was up.

The final scene of one episode (22 May 1987) has the village shopkeeper Martha Woodford attempting to seduce Freddie Danby. They are sorting through some of Freddie's old records, and Martha suddenly comes across an old one she used to dance to with her husband. The name 'Vic Miller', and the audible scratches as it starts playing, clue us into its nature as 1930s dance band music. It is this music that plays out the episode, but the peculiarity of the tune strikes the listener half way through; the 'Vic Miller' record is a reworking of *The Archers* theme tune. The programme, then, draws attention to its own status as a fiction by dissolving the theme frame which *should* mark it off from the 'real world'. Any academic literary deconstruction then becomes superfluous, and can then be used simply to make theoretical points about the nature of meaning instead of 'discovering' anything (Parker 1988b).

Action

One way of understanding the transition to postmodern architecture is to see the political ambitions of architects dashed to the ground with the old modern reform projects. There has been a rapid switch in other spheres too: from radical hopes to politicize aesthetics to desperate appeals to the potential consumers of their solutions sweetened by *aestheticizing politics*. On the British Left, for example, this has been the chosen trajectory of the new 'euro' versions of the Communist Party; designer boxer shorts sporting hammer and sickle vie for space with a filofax ('post' diaries in which, of course, the past can be taken out and conveniently thrown away) embossed with the journal's logo.

This is recuperation (the neutralization and absorption of once-radical ideas) in a new form, and works as if the activity of recuperation had itself been recuperated by the new culture. While the modern recuperation of radical political ideas works by reinterpreting them as interesting alternative opinions or suggestions for improvement, *postmodern* recuperation now consists in the representation of politics as just another representation. This is how it is possible, and not at all subversive, to walk around cities of America and Europe with carrier bags advertising 'Che Guevara' or 'Kalashinikov' boutiques, to read colour supplement articles on wine in the British Sunday newspaper the *Observer* under the heading 'Rival factions in the red brigade', or on clothing under the heading 'Militant tendency' (15 November 1987).

Attempts to maintain a sense of historical progress (a key metanarrative of modernity along with those of human science and individual meaning), which have traditionally been a part of radical political projects, are defeated by the postmodern representation of the past. These representations are so absurdly romanticized as to be useless either as a reservoir of lessons for present activity or as signposts for the direction the future might take. So, for example, the Wigan Pier Heritage Centre Shop draws tourists who have heard of the modern writer George Orwell (who combined descriptions of working-class life in the north of England with dire warnings about the dangers of bureaucracy), and sells them 'Country Kiwi Fruit & Lemon Preserve' (Hewison 1987).

With the decline of modern notions of progress or individual meaning, the descriptions do not even have the function of parodying in the service of ideals of moral or social improvement. Postmodernity is governed, instead, by the process of *pastiche*, in which the fun of using one form to evoke another is the only point of the activity. To refuse is to risk being, in words of an American mall rat, 'totally-tres-uncool'. In the language of another of the new etiquette texts a whole range of such behaviours, choices, and acts of self-presentation would simply be 'naff' (Bryson, Fitzherbert, and Legris 1983). Appalling though these descriptions may be, they capture *more* of what is happening in social interaction and experience than academic social psychology. Now most of the research in the discipline is a bit naff.

Investigation

The third metanarrative of modernity, that of human science, quickly folds once notions of progress and meaning have succumbed. This is the point where the cultural debates feed into the enterprise of social science, and then into social psychology. Old psychology and social psychology experiments have the form of the modern television intelligence quizzes. The British television programme *Mastermind* pins the contestant under the beam of a strong spotlight and the gaze of a camera to extract a measure of a knowledge of 'facts', then celebrates the abilities of the overall winner. We become, momentarily, the investigators, the occupants of the central tower of the Panopticon, and observe the activities of the prisoner in the black leather chair.

While new paradigm social psychology might seek to elicit a shared answer or elucidate the meaning of the situation from a number of contestants (as in *Ask the Family*), postmodern investigation is actually more akin to shows like *The Price is Right* where the only measure of success is how deliriously happy the winners are with their prizes. When a correct answer is required, it is superfluous; it is the guessing which is the main point of the exercise.

Approaches within microsociology, which new social psychology drew upon, show an affinity with postmodern perspectives on the self and social action. Goffman's (1971) descriptions of self-presentation, for example, treat social settings as stages, and, through the determined application of the dramaturgical metaphor, break down the distinction between the theatrical and the everyday. Goffman's sociology has been singled out as representative of the new age in which modern morality has been edged out by machiavellian social 'actors' (MacIntyre 1981). The most dramatic precursor of postmodernism in sociological social psychology, however, is ethnomethodology. The similarities I described in Chapter six between ethnomethodology and deconstruction are the basis for the link between these types of investigation and contemporary culture. The social construction of individual meaning, the power of language to undo all claims to progress, and the unravelling of the truth claims of science are common themes. Ethnomethodologists have notoriously avoided any contact with political activity which might involve the 'objectification' of social categories such as 'classes' or 'states'. Because the social world is a product, and 'accomplishment', of shared meanings of social actors, it is unknowable as a thing in itself. The thorough-going scepticism must apply equally, of course, to any proposals for alternatives made by radicals. This position paralyzes politics.

It is only recently that the enthnomethodologists involved in the sociology of science, who have inspired the new 'discourse analysis' in social psychology (Potter and Wetherell 1987) and who demonstrated that notions of replicability and falsification are rhetorical constructions, have dared to suggest an appropriate politics. This politics is explicitly presented as a variety of *pluralism*: 'postmodern pluralism recognized that it is not reality which is too complex or too rich but that there is always something more to be said' (The 2nd January Group 1986: 26). *After Truth: A Post-Modern Manifesto* turns away from the metanarratives of modernity to the little stories of the 'new age', for 'every story contains its own potentialities for progress' (ibid.: 29). Were we to move on from relativism to *reflexivity*, the manifesto contends, it would be possible to 'reinvent the world' and respond not merely theoretically by way of 'performance'.

A lesson is that when postmodernists from the social sciences do put forward a positive principle to replace the old modern nostrums, it usually boils down to the same ingredients of reflexivity, an idealized notion of conversation (with philosophy continuing the 'conversation' of the postmodern age), and pluralism served up on a linguistic base. 'Difference' is in vogue. It then all too easily sounds like a rehash of old modern liberalism which tries to pretend power does not exist by treating us all as if we were also all the same. This context, for example, allows celebrities writing in Intourist holiday brochures to allay fears about the Russians, and assert that 'they are people just like any other and, like any other, different from other people, as all people must be' (Ustinov 1988: 3).

Post-politics

There are issues which must be dealt with if social psychologists are not to end up abandoning all descriptions of power and ideology, however inadequate they might be. I will flag those issues now, and will connect them with more directly political matters relating to social psychology as an institution in the next chapter.

Inside the discipline

In terms of the representation of interaction and methods of investigation, the postmodern age is fraught with problems, Saussure's (1974) proposal, for a new 'science' that studies the life of signs in society, has been stretched to an extreme by the post-structuralist emphases on texts and discourses. A claim we meet time and again in this work is that because the organization of 'signifiers' in any tissue of meaning is self-referential, it is not possible to produce any representation of what lies outside in the 'real'. One of the characteristics of the discourse discourse in social psychology is precisely that it systematically undermines all claims to truth. Similarly, the fetish with language, and the consequent dismissal of research into the structure of power relations in the practical order of society, paralyses any action a new social psychologist

influenced by 'post' ideas might be tempted to take. The conceptual pluralism can result in a political pluralism which lets things
be. Then the investigation of interaction simply becomes a series
of pointless journalistic exercises. Social psychologists who have
followed the route out of the crisis, via ethogenics into literary
theory, then find to their chagrin that others are doing it much
more effectively outside the discipline anyway.

Outside the discipline

Three more general problems also arise as a result of the attempts
to overthrow the culture of modernity. The first concerns the
attack on the importance of the intentions of speaking 'subjects'.
While academics in literary theory might be happy to think of
themselves as 'dispersed subjects' (Young 1982), the notion of the
'death of the author' (Barthes 1977), and a simple emphasis on
discourses and texts regardless of who wrote them, cannot be
allowed to pass unchallenged. There are dire political implications in allowing others to take the place of the oppressed and to
have them speak for them if they adopt the correct terms of a
discourse. An example can be seen in the withdrawal by the
London feminist publishing house, Virago, which had to call back
and pulp 10,000 copies of a book *Down the Road, Worlds Away*
(Forward 1987) about the experiences of young Asian women in
Britain. The shy Islamic writer turned out to be a white male vicar
from Brighton. This is not, of course, to say that the problem is
postmodern prelates, but that a discourse of the postmodern which
only parodies the truth claims of modernity can also invite
academics and ex-radicals simply to play with, instead of politicize,
texts.

The second problem concerns philosophy, and political perspectives. The politics of a deconstructive strategy twists around to
deconstruct the position of the critic. The proposal that the world
consists merely of discourses then entails that radicals must recant
attachments to a truer account, admit that their own account is just
another discourse and seek solace in 'reflexivity'. We should also
be aware that simple attacks on power as 'totalitarian' are not
necessarily the property of *progressive* 'radicals'. The radical Right
is well aware of debates over the power of language, discourse,
and hegemony, and is using those notions to reconstruct the form

of popular debates over the nature of cultural and sexual 'difference' (Seidel 1986). In some forms this involves the deliberate promotion of relativism as an alternative to the old liberalism which traditionally masked various forms of right-wing discourse. This risks doing the theoretical work to underpin unwittingly a backlash *against* the political resistance to ideology and power that has been built outside the discipline. This rhetoric is then picked up, for example, to justify imperialist intervention in Latin America: the 'Santa Fé document' argues that 'Human rights which is a culturally and politically relative concept ... must be abandoned and replaced by a non-interventionist policy of political and ethical realism' (cited in Didion 1987).

Finally, there are issues to do with the geographical locations of these ideas which should signal caution. We should be aware of geographical correlates of the shift from modern to postmodern culture. It has often been said that the radicals of 1968 started their activities on the Left in Paris and conceptually migrated to end their political lives on the Right in California. The ideas have a radical European flavour, but the enthusiasts in America are able to emphasize particularly effectively, their conservative effects. The problems which post-structuralism and postmodernity pose for social psychologists, and the more general political problems which flow from those sets of ideas, need to be treated as *contradictions*, There are conflicting discourses at work as the Modern Age appears to die, and there are conflicting political responses by social psychologists to the crisis the death throes have provoked. We will explore these in the final chapter. The moral I want to draw from this chapter is that the social sciences have witnessed ideas similar to those attending the current 'post' craze before, and the positive aspects of post-structuralism must not be allowed to disappear under the popular postmodern illusion that language is free from ideology and power. The attempt to save a space for some form of 'realism' is intimately bound up with the attempt to save a space in social psychology for resistance, a refusal to respond within dominant meanings.

Chapter eight

Politics

Each alternative to the old paradigm involves a particular assessment of the cultural changes looked at in Chapter seven, and each is political. Theories in social psychology that have claimed to revolutionize the discipline have often, as a matter of course, restricted their focus to conceptual problems. Some new approaches have deliberately linked with political positions and so have raised issues addressed in this chapter. I will outline three possible political positions that have been adopted by radical social psychologists: a minimum approach, a maximum approach, and a middle way which attempts to have the best of both worlds. Each of these solutions is inadequate, In the final section I will turn to the type of politics for social psychology which *could* follow from a critical adoption of post-structuralist ideas.

Fatal attraction

The first cautious solutions to the malaise in the discipline operate on the homeopathic principle that the remedy increases in strength the less of it that is proffered. In the most daring variants of this position the rhetoric of paradigm shifts is adopted (and accepted because 'science' is thought to be improved in the process). Often, when they break from the American mainstream approach, they fall into the arms of an idealized 'European' social psychology, or appeal to work in sociology to legitimate their arguments. The minimum programmes have been extremely effective in unsettling the discipline and opening the way for more radical positions, but we should ask what the political limitations are. The clearest expositions of this position is found in ethogenic writings.

Structures of common reason

A democratic spirit spurs Harré's (1979) objections to the way orthodox social psychology continually privileges its own professional accounts over those given by the lay public. In one of the early statements of the new social psychology he champions the versions of social reality given by those who are traditionally objectified as the discipline's 'subjects': 'Everyone is, in a certain sense, a fairly competent social scientist, *and we must not treat his (or her) theory about the social world with contempt*' (Harré 1974: 244). The trouble with this is that not only are all accounts treated as valid here, but Harré also leaves a loophole open ('in a certain sense') for his own structuralist conception of the expressive order and the possibilities of changing it. There are three problems: what follows from the guarantee to respect everyone's right to give accounts; what contradiction springs from the sleight of hand which allows new social psychologists to give better accounts; and what the political position Harré suggests allows and disallows.

The 'moral standpoint' Harré presents has the overall aim of augmenting human powers of autonomy and reflexivity, and he is insistent that such powers could not be realized without 'social order' (Harré 1979). A crucial moral principle of every social order for him is that all persons should be accorded the right to speech. If Harré is serious here, then many problems would beset researchers faced with issues which demand political judgements about the effects of speech. It has been correctly pointed out, for example, that new social psychologists faced with fascist accounters would end up giving voice to, and effectively be colluding with, that politics by slipping into the trap of 'unthinking sentimentality' (Billig 1977).

At the same time, the necessary loophole in the ethogenic rhetoric opens up, as Harré makes it clear that 'in a certain sense' people do *not* know what they are doing. This is where the new social psychologist has the edge. In research practice the studies of trouble on the football-ground terraces had to account for the way in which the fans talked about their activities as being chaotic when they should have known that they were really following social rules. In this case, the solution to the problem was to resort to the claim that there was 'a conspiracy on the part of members of an orderly sub-culture to deny that order exists' (Marsh *et al.*

1974). When it comes to the theoretical elaboration of this sophistic manoeuvre, Harré appeals to his 'realistic' position: 'When the search for structure and the struggle for depth are abondoned altogether then we have the kind of monumental reaction that all but destroyed psychology as a discipline in the 1950s and 1960s' (Harré 1981b: 8). Here, of course, he is reassuring psychologists that he does not want to destroy the discipline.

The political position that emerges is effectively a conservative one, for not only do structures of meaning prevent political change, but they also ensure that radical politics is self-defeating. It is not, he says, 'in the power of human agents to have a *determinate* effect upon structural constraints, political action must be confined to the sphere of possible human action' (Harré 1979: 428). Now it turns out that not only does new social psychology study 'small-scale interactions and man-sized [sic] institutions' (Harré 1979: 348), but it defends them against the expressive system, a system he later terms the 'primary structure' (Harré 1983). The sting in the tail is that he also defends small social worlds against those who want to transform the macrostructure. He warns that well-meaning radicals operating in the 'confrontation mode' will always fail to destroy the existing social order: 'The effect of challenging it is to force its supporters to formulate their view of society more fully, thus making it more real' (Harré 1979: 399). This ethogenic politics built on 'folk theories of the social world' (Harré ibid.: 350) tips its hat towards anarchism (ibid.: 397) but looks suspiciously like old liberalism dressed up in new clothes.

Meanings of common sense

When we turn to Shotter's self-defined 'Left' version of ethogenics, we find a rhetoric which is much better, but which unfortunately folds into a similar pluralist position (though in some places he does go beyond this). One way into the politics which flows from his hermeneutic version of new social psychology is through recalling Harré's and Shotter's difference over the value of 'realism'. A 'new psychology' for Shotter, is one which should 'discover general principles by which we can transform ourselves from being victims to being masters of our fates' (Shotter 1975: 32). This is, at least, a progressive advance on Harré's position.

However, the 'personal processes' Shotter later discusses are informed by a particular use of ethnomethodology. This leads him to counterpose approaches which claim to see 'different' things to lay people to a social psychology which merely hopes to see 'more'. The chief objection is to 'the idea of experience-independent objects . . . in psychology' (Shotter 1984: 24).

On the surface, Shotter holds more firmly than Harré to the idea that the people social psychology studies should be supported in their struggle to report and account for experience. The virtue of his 'mundane realism' is that it always takes personal accounts seriously. However, there is once again a slippage from this defence of personal sense into a conservative defence of social order. Because Shotter is so sure that social activities and mental events are potentially transparent and knowable to all, he implies here that conflict and resistance are not really necessary. He reluctantly but ineluctably arrives at this position through his adoption of the accounts given by the Renaissance humanist Vico.

In a paper on the work of Vico, Shotter distances himself from his own earlier proposals for a 'moral science of action' (1975: 32). Instead (as you saw in the discussions of his response to attribution theory in Chapter four), he pessimistically diagnoses western culture as moving to a stage where we will have 'behaviour being explained by impersonal causes, and actions by reasons' (Shotter 1981b: 281). The only escape route is a return to 'common sense'. This time the sleight of hand which returns the new social psychologist to a privileged position over the struggles of lay people is not an appeal to structures of meaning but to 'deep and abstract aspects of common sense' (Shotter 1981b: 283). If this were adopted it could not be a guide for political action but would result in immediate paralysis. The grounding for common sense, for Vico, was religious mystification: 'That which regulates all human nature is the divine justice which is administered by divine providence to preserve human society' (Shotter 1981b: 272).

Star wars

An extreme response to the crisis in social psychology would be to administer poison, or simply leave it to die. One variant of this position looks to social-psychological studies carried out in countries that have overthrown capitalism. Another turns to different disciplines. The problem with this is that all too often, when idealized alternative disciplines are constructed, those who escaped quickly forget the lessons they learnt from the crisis and then reproduce the very problems which led to it. The 'radicals' then fold back into the old assumptions and practices.

'Socialist' social psychology

An object lesson here is the way that Russian social psychology appears to be an alternative to, but is actually a reproduction of, the traditional experimental social psychology. The history of social psychology in Russia shows some significant similarities to that of the discipline in the West. The precursors of social psychology were to be found in the development of a 'folk psychology'. This research was carried out under the auspices of the Russian Geographical Society (eventually in a sub-discipline called psychological ethnography). Like Wundt, whose work was developed at roughly the same time in Germany, this folk psychology studied folk tales, songs, proverbs, riddles, and legends. The role of language in thought was emphasized. Thousands of 'observers' throughout Russia collected this information. As the political situation deteriorated in the lead-up to the revolutions of 1905 and then 1917, the Russian military started to show an interest. The Academy of Military Law wanted to use the resources of social psychology to understand how people worked in crowds. The two key questions were how the members of the army could be bound together to prevent rebellion, and how the rebellious crowds outside the army be dealt with. One of the first books on military social psychology was called *How and with what are people controlled?* (cited in Budilova 1984). This crowd psychology was strikingly similar to that put forward by Le Bon (1896) and absorbed into American social psychology.

The crucial developments occurred as the bureaucracy crystallized, and the dynamic of the revolution was turned back. This is when Taylorism was a craze. Taylor's (1911) ideas had spread from America, and were taken up by the Russian engineers. The concern with the close observation, prediction, and control of behaviour was thus carried out by the scientific managers of the Soviet Union with the enthusiastic blessing of Lenin (Smith 1983). As in America, but with a different ideological gloss, a laboratory-experimental social psychology came into being. The third stage culminates in the bizarre experimental work on collective self-discipline. Chernyshev's (1984) work, for example, attempts to reveal the social psychological indexes of collective activity, to reflect managerial and organizational relationships. The 'Group Sensorimotor Integrator' measures the ability of a group of seven to move a stylus along an S-shaped maze. When the stylus touches the wall of the maze a stressor, an unpleasantly loud noise, is sent through a pair of headphones.

What is different about the Soviet approach is that while American social psychology reflects its own culture's obsession with individuals and prefers to measure their behaviour in the laboratory, in this study the work is carried out in groups. The similarity, of course, is that the machine in the laboratory operates as a disciplinary device. The Soviet state is favourable to collective action but is as reluctant as the American social psychologists to let it get out of control. Soviet social psychology is interested in understanding the behaviour of groups, but only so it can assist the state in controlling them (either by disciplining them or getting them to discipline themselves). In this respect, social psychology is used to further state control of social life (Billig 1982).

Eventually, we come full circle, and can see how conservative this disciplinary, laboratory-experimental social psychology actually is, when European social psychologists meet those influenced by the Russian ideas. Having spent much time combating the influence of American social psychology, West Europeans have been dismayed to find the same approach emanating from supposedly socialist countries. In Eastern Europe, where there are contacts with 'European social psychologists', there are also, by all accounts, deep theoretical conflicts. Hungary is a good example of this, as it has been more open to ideas from the West. At the 1972 Hungarian Social Psychological Conference, for example, there were conflicts between the people influenced by the Marxists of the French school, such as Plon (1974) and the more traditional 'conservative' Hungarian group. The latter seemed to spend much of their time experimentally examining a 'production-centred' psychological approach to decisions using groups playing 'Monopoly' (Garai *et al.* 1979).

Anti-social psychology

I showed in Chapter five how social representations theory appeals to sociology but ends up importing dubious conceptions of the individual and the social. One of the most extreme cases of the wholesale rejection of any engagement with social psychology, for example, is that of the ethnomethodologists. They appear to reject everything but end up, in practice, flipping back into a position which is blind to the operations of power and ideology (because it cannot bring itself to accept that those phenomena exist). The turn to rhetoric and to the role of conversation as the touchstone of an alternative social psychology treads just such a path. If what goes on between people is idealized as a rehash of the old humanist sentimentalizing of individuals, then descriptions of conflict or resistance drop out of the picture.

Even in literary theory, where the post-structuralist ideas discussed in this book have come to fruition, the deliberate rejection of psychology has not produced a thorough, radical account of social action. There have been tantalizing suggestions about the role of meaning and the positioning of people as 'subjects' in texts and discourses, but this work has all too quickly burnt itself out in the fires of fashion. The main enemy was eventually taken to be theory itself (Young 1982). Literary theorists bored with Derrida and Foucault are either collapsing back into versions of humanism or are turning to reductionist and positivist solutions. Now even old-paradigm social psychologists, tutored in theories of meaning by the structuralists in their own discipline could happily pick up a text and work with a 'reader reception' theorist to discover the interpretations that an individual in an audience was picking up (Eagleton 1983).

True stories

A third, middle-way approach attempts to combine a soothing bedside manner with urgent proposals for drastic surgery to save social psychology. Here the contradictions emerge, of course, for this looks very much like traditional medicine. Perhaps this is too jaundiced a view, for I would include here those approaches that have done most to make 'discourse' a research topic. There are two variants that have succeeded in this endeavour, but so far they have not connected adequately with a political practice for radicals dissatisfied with the state of the discipline. Two positions stood poised to pull social psychology beyond ethogenic critiques of laboratory-experimentation. One tradition turned to 'discourse analysis' in social psychology, while the other attempted to 'change the subject' in psychology. We should critically consider the fate of each.

After new social psychology

The first of the traditions comes from ethnomethodology and the sociology of science. It has now found its voice in a textbook of critique and methodology. Potter and Wetherell's (1987) *Discourse and Social Psychology* has succeeded in imposing a particular 'political' agenda on radicals in social psychology. The book has been heralded as 'a significant step toward a post-modern psychology' (Gergen in the publisher's blurb), and in certain respects it is. It uses scientists' discourse to show how it is not their 'facts' but their *rhetorics* which give research its credibility, and this has the useful effect of undermining the effects of positivism in social psychology. The book shows how accounts can be understood as 'interpretive repertoires', and provides the semblance of a method for an anti-positivist to display regularities in data without appealing to the traditional humanist touchstones of intention and personal meaning.

The problems and limitations of *Discourse and Social Psychology*, however, flow from the definition the authors give of their object of inquiry. In this respect, they depart markedly from the definitions of discourse which were given by writers in the post-structuralist tradition outside social psychology at the end of the 1960s (when conceptual and political crises broke out inside and outside the academic world). However, because their definition of discourse was that it was 'all forms of spoken interaction, formal or informal, and written texts of all kinds' (Potter and Wetherell 1987: 6), an account of the systematic and coercive nature of discourse was lost. Discourses, as Foucault (1972) argued, have a 'reality' and an organization beyond the individual. Once we take this step we are in a position to uncover the way discourses follow and reproduce the contours of power relations. The discourses position 'subjects'.

After the subject

The definition given of discourse in this book is closer to the notion of discourse offered by an influential representative of the second of the two traditions which could have dislodged both the old and new paradigms from their position in social psychology. *Changing the Subject* came out of post-structuralist revisions of political theory and semiology, and presented a politically more radical critique of psychology. For its writers, discourse is 'any regulated system of statements' (Henriques *et al*. 1984: 105). The line of work in this book follows the British journal *Ideology and Consciousness* which appeared briefly at the end of the 1970s, and which was an important conduit for Foucauldian ideas into psychology and sociology (Adlam *et al*. 1977).

The Henriques *et al*. (1984) book is also a manifestation of postmodernity. The description of feelings, for example, given in the chapter on heterosexual relationships, embeds those feelings in discourse. The notion of 'love' is interpreted as being recirculated in discourse and evoking issues of power, dependency and vulnerability. It is what saying 'I love you' accomplishes, the *effects* it has, and the way it positions subjects that defines what 'love' is. The risk, again, is that we become drawn into a spiral of linguistic reflexivity which is present in all postmodern culture. Concepts of 'progress', 'scientific psychology', and individual 'meaning' are attacked, with the last one of these subjected to a sophisticated psychoanalytic critique of the 'subject'. What needs to be added, though, is more than the implicit politics which those who followed the *Ideology and Consciousness* debates know about. An explicit political programme for social psychology needs to be formulated.

After American social psychology

In American social psychology the descriptions of a postmodern age have already been taken up by radicals who led a movement against laboratory-experimentation very similar to that of the new social psychologists. The ideas of deconstruction discussed by Sampson (1983) have been turned against the notion of the individual so beloved of the dominant culture in America since social psychology began. Gergen's (1973) argument that social psychological phenomena change so rapidly that it is impossible to produce 'facts' about enduring processes is often cited in the new

149

paradigm literature. It is even hoped that this will lead to a study of texts and the development of a 'postmodern psychology' (Shotter and Gergen 1988). In these formulations, Shotter's ethogenic positon becomes radicalized, and more useful to political critiques of the discipline.

The turn to discourse in radical British and American social psychology, and the abandonment of the old modern metanarratives of human science, individual meaning, and progress, have caught the enthusiasts in the pluralist vice. If every statement about the nature of social-psychological method or theory can be glossed as rhetorical device, and if all truth claims are just sophistic tricks, then how can the analysis of discourse be put to progressive use? I am *not* suggesting that the practitioners of discourse analysis, for example, think that the elaboration of different discourses is sufficient. The problem is that they have argued so strongly for the importance of discourse without integrating an account of its practical and political contexts, that when they claim it is not sufficient, social psychologists can interpret the claim as being another disclaimer, or ironic speech act.

The trap each of these has fallen into is that they have started from the premise that the crucial struggle is the one to be waged at the level of theory and method within the discourse of social psychology. Issues to do with the steps social psychologists should follow or the nature of signification are important, but not sufficient. The attempts to balance between a cautious approach which does not upset anybody and an extreme rejection of every assumption which holds social psychology together are useful object lessons for those of us who do want to connect theory and politics. Instead of reconstructing, we need to *deconstruct* social psychology (Shotter and Parker 1989).

Back to the future

Social psychology can be deconstructed if you hold on to the idea that social psychology enjoys the little power that is given to it in the academic world, and reproduces the ideologies that feed it, not only because it is a set of theories circulating in the expressive sphere but also because it is a network of institutions laced into the practical order of society. The politics needed must develop in relation to the institutions as well as the ideas and methods which give them meaning. This politics has also to refuse to balance between complete acceptance of social psychology and a wholesale rejection of it. Instead, a series of dynamics have to be set up which will continually change the discipline. To do that we have to turn to the strengths of those outside by turning over agendas for research and empowering those who have often only experienced the discipline when they have been subjected by it.

Past the post

The descriptions of postmodernity are important, for the post-structuralist concerns with language have found expression *for some* in parts of western culture. What these descriptions must not be allowed to obscure, however, is that the culture we have been describing is the *dominant* culture, not just one among many that compete equally in the world market. Just as discourses conflict with one another and participate in patterns of oppression and resistance, so cultures reproduce the effects of power relations in the texts which hold them together. It is telling to step back from the debates over the nature of modernity and postmodernity for a moment to reflect on the way all definitions of 'social psychology' are bound into power relations. We can do this by considering the fate of social psychology in countries outside America and Europe which are, as a matter of course, significantly absent from the crisis literature.

Situating social psychology in an international context also has the function of connecting the expressive order with physical, economic, and practical distribution of power in society. It is not accidental, of course, that social psychologies outside America and Europe often interpret their own progress through these dominant paradigms. I can only start to explain this by extending the histories of social psychology discussed so far in this book to the Third World. I will take the case of social psychology in Africa as the main point of reference, for this raises many issues new social psychology has discussed about rights to account for all.

The development of social psychology has to be situated in the context of the colonialization of Africa. This process of division also affected the colonialist perceptions of the native population. These concerns structured psychology when it found its way into the colonies, and then determined the shape of social psychology.

Not surprisingly, a liberal rationale could be given for research. Among the reasons given for carrying out studies of Bushmen in the 1970s, for example, was that studying 'earlier ways of human life' would bring problems of modern 'civilization into perspective', that experimental study would help improve methods, that studying 'earlier stages of intellectual endeavour' would clarify what intelligence is (and resolve the nativist/empiricist controversy). The final reason was that the results could be beneficial to the Bushmen. In short, the African became a convenient guinea pig for the self-understanding of Europeans (Bulhan 1981). William McDougall was among those who enthused over work on the mentality of Africans and saw the results as pointing the way for practical policies for dealing with them.

All histories should be, as Foucault reminds us, histories of the present structured for present purposes, and this history immediately raises questions about the continuing use of social psychology in the African continent, and in particular the way it is relayed, from America and Europe through the South African state. This raises questions of political choice. Inside South Africa social psychologists find themselves unable to do 'neutral' research. Either they end up collecting information for the state and acting as witting or unwitting public relations persons for apartheid (in research carried out on 'social development' in Namibia, for example), or they collect information against the state and risk imprisonment. Work on South African police torture of black detainees can only be carried out with the co-operation of the resistance groups and leads to the harassment of those responsible (Foster 1987). This work also raises questions about the right of all to account, and what the effects are of allowing academics from South Africa to talk about some innocuous area of social psychology and give the impression that everything is 'normal'. Accounts given in this context would have the function of glossing over the significance of conflict and repressing the voices of those in South Africa who are not allowed to speak. Were we to refuse to raise questions about black resistance here, we too would be participating in the reproduction of power. (This book will not be sold in South Africa.)

Taking the power

Those aspects of new social psychology and of post-structuralist work on discourse that are useful for an understanding of power and ideology should be taken up, but this selective appropriation of ideas runs both ways. New social psychology has succeeded in presenting ideas to an academic audience that have themselves been borrowed. An essential source for the turn from positivist research done on 'subjects' to qualitative work with accountees was the development of feminist critiques of social 'science'. In sociology this has found expression in the research close to ethnomethodology (Stanley and Wise 1983). In social psychology in Britain the development of alternatives to laboratory experimentation has carried on alongside, but independently of, new social psychology (Wilkinson 1986). What feminist critics are now doing is turning their attention to the way that women can work within the *institutional* constraints of a male-dominated discipline and raise questions about what the practice of psychology by feminists should be like (Burman 1989). Feminists are also connecting deconstruction with political critique (Squire 1989).

Traditionally, the agendas for research have been set within the institutions, and when social problems have been addressed they have been held at a distance so that the 'subjects' become seen, in some sense, as the source of the problem. The institutional changes which are most important are those which set up *dynamics* in which the 'subjects' become empowered, become able to determine what research would be relevant. Such political dynamics are risky and, for some traditional social psychologists, threatening. They are all the more unnerving because they would involve giving up power and taking off from immediate political concerns developing outside the safety of the psychology department. For example, in Britain at the time of writing, a clause of the local government act aims to prevent some social psychologists from supporting the resistance of gay men and lesbians to discrimination and exposing theories which treat their sexuality as abnormal. While the new social psychological insistence that everybody should be allowed to 'account' is relevant here, it is hardly sufficient.

In the account of the early history of social psychology I gave in Chapter two, I focused on the repression which accompanied the birth of the discipline, a repression intimately connected with culture and with class. These issues are still crucial, and every challenge to the cultural and gender dominance in social psychology is also a challenge to its class basis. Reading between the lines, accounts of the work carried out in countries still directly and militarily threatened by imperialism in Latin America, involve social psychologists in political activity. In Latin America, for example, the criteria for good research are bound up with the empowering of the local community. The questions set by the community have to be addressed, and the 'social psychologists' who work in teams adopt a supportive role. This often brings them into head-on conflict with the state (Marin 1983). After the Mexico City earthquake, for example, the work teams facilitating the reconstruction of the community found themselves having to make political choices about *whose* power would be deconstructed, and whose power would be developed. In cases like these, the political role of the 'researcher' starts to dissolve her identity as 'social psychologist': the whole history and political function of the discipline starts to unravel.

Fourteen rules for radicals

New social psychology claims that in 'exceptional circumstances' the expressive order can be radically altered through changes to the practical order. I want to take this seriously, and suggest some steps that could be taken now to intervene at both levels. These points serve to summarize some of the ideas discussed in this book. Some of these measures, rules for radicals to adopt in the everyday subversion of social psychology, operate purely at the expressive level, but most will also involve deeper changes in the discipline.

1: Perception. Social psychology is particularly amenable to post-structuralist ideas because it is concerned with a level of social organization where there is no truth. So, *do not take anything as fact*. All the 'facts' are culturally and historically specific. Their functions as deceptions should be opposed.

2: Progress. Phrasing which refers to 'finding' and 'discovering' things not only link into a scientific notion of truth, but also a particular notion of scientific progress. So, *avoid metaphors of revelation when they are applied to 'facts' about social interaction.*

3: Politics. If you accept that there is no 'truth' in social psychology, you have to use different criteria from the usual 'validity' game (which just wants to see how far the reactionary implications of a theory or its data link back into an equally reactionary common sense). So, *evaluate results, not in terms of what they say but in terms of what their effects are.*

4: Topics. Radical research does not necessarily arise from 'social problems', but has to be conducted from the standpoint of those who resist power. So, *think about who you want to help politically, and get them to formulate research goals.*

5: Objective style. Beware of an accumulation of references in academic papers. The presence of a host of references in a text either indicates that the writer is less critical, or that they are trying to advance contentious political points. So, although this is counter-intuitive, *disbelieve points backed up by many references.*

6: Subjective style. Beware of the use of 'I think' by eminent figures in social psychology. This reflects and reproduces social status positions (in which those higher up give their 'thoughts' (in a style closer to 'speech'), and the minions have to offer 'facts' (in objective 'written' form). You can deconstruct this if you *treat spoken discussions of social psychology as seriously as the written ones.*

7: Gender. Works which raise the question of 'sex differences' and work which ignores them are equally symptomatic of a neglect of the way difference is rarely understood as dominance. The problem does not only lie in the data, so *ask what it is about the theory, and the language used to describe it, that is gendered.*

8: History. It is not enough to present a history of the research topic, but the method used, and the theory chosen, should also be interrogated. *Link the method and the theory with cultural changes, and say who would object to it, and why.*

9: Arguing. It is generally assumed that once 'enough' social psychology (or psychology) has been absorbed, we will all think the same. Against that, we should argue that the more we know, the more the contradictions open up between opponents in the discipline. So, in order to facilitate spaces for resistance, *research and teaching sessions should open up the conflicts for the audience to see.*

10: Rhetoric. Radicals should allow their political concerns to structure their social-psychological theory. Think of ways to redescribe the development of social-psychological models in the terminology of radical politics, and *develop, instead of suppressing, the metaphors of conflict and resistance you use outside the discipline.*

11: Community. Talk of 'showing', 'demonstrating', and 'revealing' things appeals to the metaphor of revelation. To say that someone argues a point, or 'says' this or that, however, does not fall into this trap, and it acknowledges that opponents will always accept or reject ideas on the basis of who puts them forward. So, *explicitly refer to others' arguments, and so make the alliances and the conflicts between political positions visible.*

12: Activity. Research in psychology should also be explicitly driven by political concerns, and social psychology should be viewed as the occasion for thinking through those concerns. Avoid the temptation to 'apply' social psychological theory outside. You can 'deconstruct' the division between what is inside and what is outside social psychology by ensuring that *you are the participant observer when you are inside social psychology.*

13: Knowledge. The model of 'expertise' should be thrown into question not only at the beginning of the research, but also at the end. Where are the results published, and why? *Ask what the practical effects of research and teaching topics are on the ability of the oppressed to address political issues.*

14: Reflection. Turn the methods and theories in on psychology so that it is the theorist, not the subject, who is seen as 'abnormal'. You can deconstruct the opposition between the normal and the pathological, when you *make the meetings, seminars and teaching sessions the object of research as 'social problems'.*

None of these proposals on their own will unsettle social psychology, but if they are all adopted this will carry through in practical ways the theoretical deconstruction advanced in this book. Then we can look forward to the end of the crisis, through the end of the practices which make up modern social psychology.

Further reading

Here are some suggestions to guide you into the literature on (1) the crisis and new social psychology, (2) deconstruction, (3) the analysis of discourse, and (4) descriptions of postmodernity. These books and articles will be found more fully referenced in the reference section to this book. The dates for all the main theoretical works given in this book, and in the references, are those for the first publication in English. This is deliberate, for these are the versions employed by radicals in social psychology, and the ones available to readers wanting to follow up the ideas. (As post-structuralism points out, there are no 'originals' where you will find the 'true' meaning.)

The crisis

The manifesto for the new paradigm is Harré and Second's (1972) *The Explanation of Social Behaviour*. Harré takes a realist position, and so he is able to argue persuasively that if we treated people 'as if they were human beings' we would be being more scientific. This is not light reading, though, and a more accessible introduction to the new paradigm is contained in Harré, Clarke and De Carlo's (1985) *Motives and Mechanisms*. Harré's most interesting accounts of what new social psychology involves for social study and political change can be found in his *Social Being* (1979) and *Personal Being* (1983). There is a third volume of this projected trilogy, *Physical Being*, promised in the near future. An account of the other, hermeneutic, side of the new social psychology will be found in Shotter's (1975) *Images of Man in Psychological Research*. This is a useful thin book and is more polemical than the more recent *Social Accountability and Selfhood* (1984) which collects scattered papers together, and threads them on a narrative which is more critical than the humanism which informed Shotter's writings in the early 1970s. The more immediately political side to the crisis is represented in Armistead's (1974) edited collection *Reconstructing Social Psychology*. There are useful papers by Harré and Shotter in this volume. Although the overall themes of the book are influenced by phenomenology and humanism, the political contributions are still as useful now as they were then (and clearer than most of what I try to say). The political dynamic of the Armistead book should be continued in a forthcoming edited collection I am putting together with John Shotter called *Deconstructing Social Psychology*.

Deconstruction

The clearest account of Derrida's deconstruction of texts is to be found in Norris's (1982) *Deconstruction*. The sub-title 'Theory and practice' has attracted some criticism for implying that it is possible to maintain a distinction between the two things, but it is a useful way into a difficult area. Derrida deconstructs just such an opposition in the three interviews collected in *Positions* (1981). It would be best to begin reading him here after secondary sources, and before plunging into *Of Grammatology* (1976) which is difficult at times. Derrida should be seen in context. He can be understood in relation to literature, history, and philosophy. An accessible account of contemporary uses of deconstructions by radicals in English literature which sets Derrida (and Foucault) in the context of other approaches to texts is Eagleton's (1983) *Literary Theory*.

Discourse

It is best to read Foucault before turning to second-hand accounts of his work. *The History of Sexuality I* (1981) is an acute, poetic, and (paradoxically) liberating analysis of discourses of sexuality and practices of confession. Then turn to *Discipline and Punish* (1977). This was written as part of a political campaign in France in the early 1970s in support of prisoners. The analysis of discourse Foucault provides is represented in psychology in Henriques *et al.*

Changing the Subject (1984). This is heavy going in places, but some of the chapters connect with themes in this book and are useful guides to research. A more politically cautious use of the notion of 'discourse' is to be found in Potter and Wetherell's (1987) *Discourse and Social Psychology*. Anyone who is tempted to do research on discourses should read this book. The 'ten steps' to analysis can be taken with a pinch of salt, but they can be used as part of the presentational rhetoric to get work through institutional barriers.

Postmodernity

Perhaps because it is all around us, it is all the more difficult to identify postmodernism. You might like to listen to Talking Heads' music and reflect on whether there is any real meaning to be drawn out of the songs (unlike traditional love songs, for example, which appeal to 'deep' common feelings). The easiest way into this is Hewison's (1987) *The Heritage Industry*, in which he gives an account of how the 'past' has become constructed for present purposes. A sense of history has been erased as romanticized disneyesque snapshots take over the museum service. The first theoretical piece to read should be Fredric Jameson's chapter in Foster's *Postmodern Culture* (1985). (The book was first published in America under the title *The Anti-Aesthetic*.) Jameson at least tries to hold on to a radical political position, unlike Lyotard in *The Postmodern Condition* (1984). Lyotard's book is not easy to read, but it is short. It helps to begin with the interview at the end of the book. An overall philosophical appraisal of Derrida, Foucault, and Lyotard which also traces through their affiliations to psychoanalysis, is Peter Dews's (1987) *Logics of Disintegration*. This is difficult, but after the other books it provides a framework for these complex ideas. I found a way into post-structuralism through Dews's work, and *after* you have looked at the other reading you could use his book to find your way out the other side.

References

Adams, D. (1977) *The Hitch-Hiker's Guide to the Galaxy*, London: Pan.

Adams, D. and Lloyd, J. (1983) *The Meaning of Liff*, London: Pan.

Adlam, D., Henriques, J., Rose, N., Salfield, A., Venn, C., and Walkerdine, V. (1977) 'Psychology, ideology and the human subject', *Ideology and Consciousness* 1: 5–56.

Allport, F. H. (1919) 'Behaviour and experiment in social psychology', *Journal of Abnormal and Social Psychology* 14: 297–306.

Allport, F. H. (1927) 'The present status of social psychology', *Journal of Abnormal and Social Psychology* 21: 373–83.

Allport, G. W. (1968) 'The historical background of modern social psychology', in G. Lindzey and E. Aronson (eds) *The Handbook of Social Psychology I* (2nd edn), Massachusetts: Addison-Wesley.

Althusser, L. (1971) *Lenin and Philosophy and Other Essays*, London: New Left Books.

Armistead, N. (ed.) (1974) *Reconstructing Social Psychology*, Harmondsworth: Penguin.

Asch, S. E. (1952) *Social Psychology*, New Jersey: Prentice-Hall.

Austin, J. L. (1956) 'A plea for excuses', in V. C. Chappell (ed.) (1981) *Ordinary Language: Essays in Philosophical Method*, New York: Dover Publications Inc.

Barthes, R. (1977) *Image–Music–Text*, London: Fontana.

Bem, D. J. (1972) 'Self-perception theory', *Advances in Experimental Social Psychology* 6: 1–62.

Bentley, M. (1937) 'The nature and uses of experiment in psychology', *American Journal of Psychology* 50: 452–69.

Berger, P. L. and Luckmann, T. (1971) *The Social Construction of Reality: a Treatise in the Sociology of Knowledge*, Harmondsworth: Penguin.

Bernard, L. L. (1936) 'Review of H. Gurnee's *Elements of Social Psychology*', *American Sociological Review* 1: 829–30.

Billig, M. (1977) 'The new social psychology and "fascism"', *European Journal of Social Psychology* 7: 393–432.

Billig, M. (1982). *Ideology and Social Psychology: Extremism. Moderation and Contradiction*, Oxford; Basil Blackwell.

Billig, M. (1985) 'Prejudice, categorization and particularization: from a perceptual to a rhetorical approach', *European Journal of Social Psychology* 15: 79–103.

Billig, M. (1987) *Arguing and Thinking: a rhetorical approach to social psychology*, Cambridge: Cambridge University Press.

Blum, A. and McHugh, P. (1971) 'The social ascription of motives', *American Sociological Review* 36: 98–109.

Boring, E. G. (1929) *A History of Experimental Psychology*, London: The Century Co.

———— (1968) 'Edwin Garrigues Boring', in E. G. Boring, H. S. Langfield, H. Werner, and R. M. Yerkes (eds) *A History of Psychology in Autobiography I*, New York: Russell & Russell.

Britt, S. H. (1937) 'Social psychologists or psychological sociologists – which?', *Journal of Abnormal and Social Psychology* 32: 314–18.

Bryson, K., Fitzherbert, S., and Legris, J.–L. (1983) *The Complete Naff Guide*, London: Arrow.

Budilova, E. A. (1984) 'On the history of social psychology in Russia', in L. Strickland (ed.) *Directions in Soviet Social Psychology*, New York: Springer-Verlag.

Bulhan, H. A. (1981) 'Psychological research in Africa', *Race and Class* 23 (1): 25–41.

Burman, E. (1989) *The Practice of Psychology by Feminists*, London: Sage.

Chernyshev, A. S. (1984) 'Experimental research on self-discipline of collectives of pupils and school children', in L. Strickland (ed.) *Directions in Soviet Social Psychology*, New York: Springer-Verlag.

Coulter, J. (1979) *The Social Construction of Mind*, London: Macmillan.

Danziger, K. (1979) 'The positivist repudiation of Wundt', *Journal of the History of the Behavioural Sciences* 15: 205–30.

Dashiell, J. F. (1930) 'The influence of competition on performance: an experimental study', *Journal of Abnormal Psychology and Social Psychology* 19: 236–53.

Davis, M. (1980) 'Why the US working class is different', *New Left Review* 123: 3–44.

Dennis, W. (1948) 'The new social psychology', in University of Pittsburgh (eds) *Current Trends in Social Psychology*, Pittsburgh: University of Pittsburgh Press.

Derrida, J. (1973) *Speech and Phenomena, and Other Essays on Husserl's Theory of Signs*, Evanston: Northwestern University Press.

Derrida, J. (1976) *Of Grammatology*, Baltimore: Johns Hopkins University Press.

Derrida, J. (1978) *Writing and Difference*, London: Routledge & Kegan Paul.

Derrida, J. (1980) 'An interview', *The Literary Review* 14: 21–2.

Derrida, J. (1981) *Positions*, London: Athlone Press.

Derrida, J. (1982) *Margins of Philosophy*, Sussex: Harvester Press.

Dews, P. (1987) *Logics of Disintegration: Post-structuralist Thought and the Claims of Critical Theory*, London: Verso.

Didion, J. (1987) *Miami*, New York: Simon & Schuster.

Durkheim, E. (1938) *The Rules of Sociological Method*, Chicago: University of Chicago Press.

Durkheim, E. (1953) 'Individual and collective representations', in E. Durkheim *Sociology and Philosophy*, London: Cohen & West.

Eagleton, T. (1983) *Literary Theory: an Introduction*, Oxford: Basil Blackwell.

Eco, U. (1986) *Travels in Hyper-reality*, London: Pan.

Farr, R. M. (1980) 'Homo socio-psychologicus', in A. J. Chapman and D. M. Jones (eds) *Models of Man*, Leicester: British Psychological Society.

Farr, R. M. (1981) 'The social origins of the human mind: a historical note', in J. Forgas (ed.) *Social Cognition: Perspectives on Everyday Understanding*, London: Academic Press.

Farr, R. M. (1984) 'Social representations: their role in the design and execution of laboratory experiments', in R. M. Farr and S. Moscovici (eds) *Social Representations*, Cambridge: Cambridge University Press.

Farr, R. M. and Moscovici, S. (1984) *Social Representations*, Cambridge: Cambridge University Press.

Filmer, P. (1972) 'On Harold Garfinkel's ethnomethodology', in P. Filmer, M. Phillipson, D. Silverman, and D. Walsh, *New Directions in Sociological Theory*, London: Collier/Macmillan.

Finison, L. J. (1976) 'Unemployment, politics, and the history of organized psychology', *American Psychologist* 31: 747–55.

Finison, L. J. (1977) 'Psychologists and Spain: a historical note', *American Psychologist* 32: 1080–4.

Fiske, S. T. and Taylor, S. E. (1984) *Social Cognition*, Reading, Mass.: Addison-Wesley.

Forgas, J. (1981) *Social Cognition: Perspectives on Everyday Understanding*, London: Academic Press.

Forward, T. (1987) *Down the Road, Worlds Away*, London: Virago.

Foster, D. (1987) *Detention and Torture in South Africa*, London: James Currey.

Foster, H. (1985) *Postmodern Culture*, London: Pluto Press.

Foucault, M. (1970) *The Order of Things*, London: Tavistock Press.

Foucault, M. (1972) *The Archeology of Knowledge*, London: Tavistock.

Foucault, M. (1977) *Discipline and Punish*, London: Allen Lane.

Foucault, M. (1981) *The History of Sexuality I: an Introduction*, Harmondsworth: Penguin.

Garai, L., Erös, F., Járó, K., Köcski, M., and Veres, S. (1979) 'Towards a social psychology of personality: development and current perspectives of a school of social psychology in Hungary', *Social Science Information* 18 (1): 137–66.

Garfinkel, H. (1967) *Studies in Ethnomethodology*, New York: Prentice-Hall.

Gauld, A. O. and Shotter, J. (1977) *Human Action and its Psychological Investigation*, London: Routledge & Kegan Paul.

Gergen, K. J. (1973) 'Social psychology as history', *Journal of Personality and Social Psychology* 26: 309–20.

Goffman, E. (1971) *The Presentation of Self in Everyday Life*, London: Penguin.

Gouldner, A. (1972) *The Coming Crisis of Western Sociology*, London: Heinemann.

Hall, G. S. (1919) 'Some possible effects of the war on American psychology', *Psychological Bulletin* 16: 48–9.

Harré, R. (1977) 'The self in monodrama', in T. Mischel (ed.) *The Self: Psychological and Philosophical Issues*, Oxford: Basil Blackwell.

Harré, R. (1979) *Social Being: a Theory for Social Psychology*, Oxford: Basil Blackwell.

Harré, R. (1980) 'Man as rhetorician', in A. J. Chapman and D. M. Jones (eds) *Models of Man*, Leicester: British Psychological Society.

Harré, R. (1981a) 'Expressive aspects of descriptions of others', in C. Antaki (ed.) *The Psychology of Ordinary Explanations of Social Behaviour*, London: Academic Press.

Harré, R. (1981b) 'The positivist-empiricist approach and its alternative', in P. Reason and J. Rowan (eds) *Human Inquiry: a Sourcebook of New Paradigm Research*, New York: Wiley.

Harré, R. (1983) *Personal Being: a Theory for Individual Psychology*, Oxford: Basil Blackwell.

Harré, R. (1985) 'Review of *Social Representations*', *British Journal of Psychology* 76: 138–40.

Harré, R., Clarke, D., and De Carlo, N. (1985) *Motives and Mechanisms: an Introduction to the Psychology of Action*, London: Methuen.

Harré, R. and Secord, P. (1972) *The Explanation of Social Behaviour*, Oxford: Basil Blackwell.

Harvey, J. H. (1981) 'Do we need another gloss on "attribution theory"', *British Journal of Social and Clinical Psychology* 20: 301–4.

Heelas, P. and Lock, A. (eds) (1981) *Indigenous Psychologies: the Anthropology of the Self*, London: Academic Press.

Heider, F. (1958) *The Psychology of Interpersonal Relations*, New York: Wiley.

Heider, F. (1976) 'A conversation with Fritz Heider', in J. H. Harvey, W. J. Ickes, and R. F. Kidd (eds) *New Directions in Attribution Research I*, Hillsdale, New Jersey: Erlbaum.

Henriques, J., Hollway, W., Urwin, C., Venn, C., and Walkerdine, V. (1984) *Changing the Subject: Psychology, Social Regulation and Subjectivity*, London: Methuen.

Herzlich, C. (1983) *Health and Illness: a Social Psychological Analysis*, London: Academic Press.

Hewison, R. (1987) *The Heritage Industry*, London: Methuen.

Icheiser, G. (1949) 'Misunderstandings in human relations: a study in false social perception', supplement to September issue of *American Journal of Sociology*, Chicago: University of Chicago Press.

J.A.S.P. (1921) 'Editorial announcement', *Journal of Abnormal and Social Psychology* 16: 1–5.

Jencks, C. (1977) *The Language of Post-Modern Architecture*, New York: Rizzoli.

Jones, E. E. and Davis, K. E. (1965) 'From acts to dispositions: the attribution process in person perception', *Advances in Experimental Social Psychology* 2: 220–66.

Jones, E. E. and Nisbett, R. E. (1971) 'The actor and the observer: divergent perceptions of the causes of behavior', in E. E. Jones, D. E. Kanouse, H. H. Kelley, R. E. Nisbett, S. Valins, and B. Weiner (eds) *Attribution: perceiving the causes of behavior*, Morristown, New Jersey: General Learning Press.

Kamin, L. (1974) *The Science and Politics of IQ*, Harmondsworth: Penguin.

Karier, C. J. (1977) 'Testing for order and control in the corporate liberal state', in N. Block and G. Dworkin (eds) *The IQ Controversy: Critical Readings*, London: Quartet.

Kelley, H. H. (1967) 'Attribution theory in social psychology', *Nebraska Symposium on Motivation* 15: 192–238.

Kuhn, T. S. (1970) *The Structure of Scientific Revolutions* (2nd edn), Chicago: University of Chicago Press.

Lamal, P. A. (1983) 'A cogent critique of epistemology leaves radical behaviourism unscathed', *Behaviourism* 11: 103–8.

Lamb, D. (1979) *Language and Perception in Hegel and Wittgenstein*, London: Avebury.

Le Bon, G. (1986) *The Crowd: a study of the Popular Mind*, London: Ernest Benn Ltd.

Lévi-Strauss, C. (1966) *The Savage Mind*, London: Weidenfeld & Nicolson.

Liberman, K. (1982) 'The economy of Central Australian Aboriginal expression: an inspection from the vantage point of Merleau-Ponty and Derrida', *Semiotica* 40: 267–346.

Lyotard, J.–F. (1984) *The Postmodern Condition: a Report on Knowledge*, Manchester: Manchester University Press.

McDougall, W. (1908/1948) *An Introduction to Social Psychology*, London: Methuen.

MacIntyre, A. (1981) *After Virtue: a Study in Moral Theory*, Indiana; University of Notre Dame Press.

Marin, G. (1983) 'The Latin American experience in applying social psychology to community change', in F. Blackler (ed.) *Social Psychology and Developing Countries*, Chichester: Wiley.

Marsh, P., Rosser, E., and Harré, R. (1974) *The Rules of Disorder*, London: Routledge & Kegan Paul.

Mead, G. H. (1934) *Mind, Self and Society: from the Standpoint of a Social Behaviorist*, Chicago: University of Chicago Press.

Middlemist, R. D., Knowles, E. S., and Matter, C. F. (1976) 'Personal space invasions in the lavatory: suggestive evidence for arousal', *Journal of Personality and Social Psychology* 33 (5): 541–6.

Milgram, S. (1963) 'Behavioral Study of Obedience', *Journal of Abnormal and Social Psychology* 69: 371–8.

Moscovici, S. (1972) 'Society and theory in social psychology', in J. Isreal, and H. Tajfel (eds) *The Context of Social Psychology: a Critical Assessment*, London: Academic Press.

Moscovici, S. (1973) 'Foreword', in C. Herzlich *Health and Illness: a Social Psychological Analysis*, London: Academic Press.

Moscovici, S. (1981a) 'On social representations', in J. Forgas (ed.) *Social Cognition: Perspectives on Everyday Understanding*, London: Academic Press.

Moscovici, S. (1981b) 'Foreword', in P. Heelas and A. Lock (eds) *Indigenous Psychologies: the Anthropology of the Self*, London: Academic Press.

Moscovici, S. (1982) 'The coming era of representations', in J.–P. Codol and J.–P. Leyens (eds) *Cognitive Analysis of Social Behaviour*, The Hague: Martinus Nijhoff.

Moscovici, S. (1984) 'The phenomenon of social representations', in R. M. Farr and S. Moscovici (eds) *Social Representations*, Cambridge: Cambridge University Press.

Moscovici, S. (1985) 'Comment on Potter and Litton', *British Journal of Social Psychology* 24: 91–2.

Nisbett, R. E. (1975) 'A conversation with R. E. Nisbett', in E. Krupat (ed.) *Psychology is Social*, Glenview, Ill.: Scott-Foresman & Co.

Norris, C. (1982) *Deconstruction: Theory and Practice*, London: Methuen.

O'Donnell, J. M. (1979) 'The crisis of experimentalism in the 1920s: E. G. Boring and his uses of history', *American Psychologist* 34: 289–95.

Parker, I. (1987a) 'The social status of mentalistic constructs', in W. J. Baker, M. E. Hyland, H. Van Rappard, and A. W. Staats (eds) *Current Issues in Theoretical Psychology*, Amsterdam: North-Holland.

Parker, I. (1987b) ' "Social representations": social psychology's (mis)use of sociology', *Journal for the Theory of Social Behaviour* 17 (4): 447–69.

Parker, I. (1988a) 'Discourse and power', in J. Shotter and K. Gergen (eds) *Texts of Identity*, London: Sage.

Parker, I. (1988b) 'Deconstructing accounts', C. Antaki (ed.) *Analysing Everyday Explanation: a Case-book of Methods*, London: Sage.

Parker, I. (1989) 'The abstraction and representation of social psychology', in J. Shotter and I. Parker (eds) *Deconstructing Social Psychology*, London: Routledge.

Pawley, M. (1987) 'The man who learned from Las Vegas', *Intercity*, November/December: 12–17.

Plon, M. (1974) 'On the meaning of the notion of conflict and its study in social psychology', *European Journal of Social Psychology* 4: 389–436.

Potter, J. and Wetherell, M. (1987) *Discourse and Social Psychology*, London: Sage.

Ring, K. (1967) 'Experimental social psychology: some sober questions about some frivolous values', *Journal of Experimental Social Psychology* 3: 113–23

Rorty, R. (1982) 'From philosophy to post-philosophy: an interview with Richard Rorty', *Radical Philosophy* 32: 1–4.

Sampson, E. E. (1983) 'Deconstructing Psychology's Subject', *Journal of Mind and Behaviour* 4 (2): 135–64.

Saussure, F. de (1974) *Course in General Linguistics*, London: Fontana.

Schopler, J. (1965) 'Social power', *Advances in Experimental Social Psychology* 2: 177–218.

Seidel, G. (1986) 'Right-wing discourse', in R. Levitas (ed.) *The Ideology of the New Right*, Oxford: Polity Press.

Shaver, K. G. (1975) *An Introduction to Attribution Processes*, Cambridge, Mass.: Winthrop Publishers.

Shotter, J. (1975) *Images of Man in Psychological Research*, London: Methuen.

Shotter, J. (1980) 'Action, joint action and intentionality' in M. Brenner (ed.) *The Structure of Action*, Oxford: Basil Blackwell.

Shotter, J. (1981a) 'Telling and reporting: prospective and retrospective uses of self-ascriptions', in C. Antaki (ed.) *The Psychology of Ordinary Explanations of Social Behaviour*, London: Academic Press.

Shotter, J. (1981b) 'Vico, moral worlds, accountability and personhood', in P. Heelas and A. Lock (eds) *Indigenous Psychologies: the Anthropology of the Self*, London: Academic Press.

Shotter, J. (1983) 'Hermeneutics', in R. Harré and R. Lamb (eds) *Encyclopedic Dictionary of Psychology*, Oxford: Basil Blackwell.

Shotter, J. (1984) *Social Accountability and Selfhood*, Oxford: Basil Blackwell.

Shotter, J. and Gergen, K. (eds) (1988) *Texts of Identity*, London: Sage.

Shotter, J. and Parker, I. (1989) *Deconstructing Social Psychology*, London: Routledge.

Silverman, D. and Torode, B. (1980) *The Material Word: Some Theories of Language and its Limits*, London: Routledge & Kegan Paul.

Smith, S. (1983) 'Taylorism rules OK? Bolshevism, Taylorism and the technical intelligentsia in the Soviet Union, 1917–41', *Radical Science Journal* 13: 3–27.

Smoke, K. (1935) 'The present status of social psychology in America', *Psychological Review* 42: 537–43.

Squire, C. (1989) *Significant Differences*, London: Routledge.

Stanley, L. and Wise, S. (1983) *Breaking Out: Feminist Consciousness and Feminist Research*, London: Routledge & Kegan Paul.

Taylor, F. W. (1911) *Scientific Management*, New York: Harper & Row.

The 2nd January Group (1986) *After Truth: a Post-Modern Manifesto*, London: Inventions Press.

Titchener, E. B. (1921) 'Wilhelm Wundt', *American Journal of Psychology* 32: 161–78.

Totman, R. (1979) *Social Causes of Illness*, London: Souvenir Press.

Totman, R. (1982) 'Undermining people's attributions', London: paper for British Psychological Society conference.

Triplett, N. (1898) 'The dynamogenic factors in pacemaking and competition'. *American Journal of Psychology* 9: 507–33.

Ustinov, P. (1988) 'I am a Russian of a kind', *Intourist Soviet Union Brochure*, April–October: 3.

Weber, M. (1930) *The Protestant Ethic and the Spirit of Capitalism*, London: Allen & Unwin.

Weber, M. (1967) *From Max Weber. Essays on Sociology*, Oxford: Oxford University Press.

Weber, M. (1968) *Economy and Society: an Outline of Interpretative Sociology*, New York: Bedminster Press.

Weber, S. (1982) 'The limits of professionalism', *Oxford Literary Review* 5 (1/2): 59–79.

Wilkinson, S. (1986) *Feminist Social Psychology: Developing Theory and Practice*, Milton Keynes: Open University Press.

Williamson, J. (1987) *Consuming Passions: the Dynamics of Popular Culture*, London: Marion Boyars.

Young, R. (1982) 'Post-structuralism: the end of theory', *Oxford Literary Review* 5 (1/2): 3–15.

Index

actions 22
acts 22
Adams, D. 132, 161
Adlam, D. 149, 161
Africa 151–2
Allport, F. H. 36, 40, 161
Allport, G. W. 29, 35, 42, 161
Althusser, L. 55, 103, 108, 161
America 13–15; American
    Psychological Association 14, 33,
    43; American social psychology
    13, 18–19, 30–44, 149–50;
    American Sociological
    Association 35
analytic philosophy see Austin, J.
    L.
applied psychology 30–1, 39
Archers, The 134
Armistead, N. 16, 159, 161
Asch, S. E. 13, 161
attribution theory 74–89
Austin, J. L. 20, 25, 161
Australian Aborigines 118
authoritarianism 62

Barthes, R. 55, 118, 120, 139, 161
Bem, D. J. 77, 161
Bentley, M. 44, 161
Berger, P. L. 34, 90, 161
Bernard, L. L. 35, 161
Billig, M. 27, 42, 62, 73, 79, 80, 87,
    107, 142, 146, 161, 162
Blum, A. 114, 162

Boring, E. G. 14, 30–2, 41, 162
Brill, A. A. 132
Britt, S. H. 35, 162
Bryson, K. 136, 162
Budilova, E. A. 145, 162
Bulhan, H. A. 152, 162
Burman, E. 153, 162

Changing the Subject see
    Henriques, J.
Chernyshev, A. S. 146, 162
Clarke, D. 164
class, 137, 154
Classical Age 62–3, 82–3
Coming Crisis of Western
    Sociology, The see Gouldner, A.
common sense 25, 77, 85–7, 143–4
communication 16, 24, 94–5
Comte, A. 34
conceptual phenomenology see
    Coulter, J.
consensuality 92–3
consensual universe 92–3
conflict see ideology
conversation 80, 108–9, 119
Coulter, J. 117, 162
crowds 35–7, 45, 145; The Crowd
    see Le Bon, G.
culture 17, 131–40, 151

Danziger, K. 32, 34, 162
Dashiell, J. F. 41, 162
Davis, K. E. see Jones, E. E.

Davis, M. 39, 162
deconstruction 57–60; of
  attribution theory 80–2;
  definition of 57; of ethogenic
  responses to attribution theory
  84–7; *see also* Derrida, J.
Dennis, W. 14, 162
Derrida, J. 56, 57, 61, 82, 95, 106,
  113–14, 116, 120–4, 159, 162
Dewey, J. 33, 109
Dews, P. 160, 163
Didion, J. 140, 163
discipline 63–4
discourse 61–2, 101–2, 148;
  definition of 61–2
discourse analysis *see* Potter, J.
Discourse and Social Psychology
  see Potter, J.
dramaturgy 20–2, 137; *see also*
  Goffman, E.
Durkheim, E. 34, 41, 95–9, 107,
  163

Eagleton, T. 104, 110, 120, 147,
  159, 163
Eco, U. 134, 163
epistemes 62
Erös, F. *see* Garai, L.
ethnomethodology, 111–13, 147;
  and deconstruction 113–15, 137;
  see also Garfinkel, H.
ethogenics 4–5, 20–3, 101, 142–5;
  definition of 4; *see also* new
  paradigm, new social psychology
eugenics 37, 84
Europe 15–17; European social
  psychology 13, 91; *European
  Journal of Social Psychology* 14
*Explanation of Social Behaviour,
  The*, 54; *see also* Secord, P. F.
expressive order 21, 27, 50, 106

Farr, R. M. 34, 95, 100, 163
feminism 26, 153
Filmer, P. 112, 163
Finison, L. J. 14, 43, 163
First World War 41–2
Fiske, S. T. 88, 163

Fitzherbert, S. *see* Bryson, K.
football supporters 51–2, 57,
  142
Forgas, J. 99, 163
Forward, T. 139, 163
Foster, D. 152, 163
Foster, H. 160, 163
Foucault, M. 46, 48, 53, 62–4, 73,
  82, 102, 105, 107, 114, 116, 148,
  159, 163

Garai, L. 146, 163
Garfinkel, H. 20, 111–2, 118, 163
Gauld, A. O. 54, 164
Gergen, K. J. 28, 116, 149–50, 164
gestalt 12
Goffman, E. 20, 137, 164
Gouldner, A. 115, 164
Group Sensorimotor Integrator
  146

Hall, G. S. 41–2, 164
Harré, R. 12, 16, 21–3, 25, 27, 44,
  49, 50, 52, 54, 58, 73, 78, 81, 85–
  6, 100, 104, 109, 142–3, 158, 164;
  see also Marsh, P.
Harvard 31
Harvey, J. H. 76, 164
Heelas, P. 28, 116, 164
Hegel, G. W. F. 109
Heidegger, M. 109
Heider, F. 73–4, 76–7, 164
Henriques, J. 105, 159, 164; *see
  also* Adlam, D.
hermeneutics 53–5
Herzlich, C. 101, 164
Hewison, R. 136, 160, 164
*History of Experimental
  Psychology, The see* Boring,
  E. G.
*Human Action and Its
  Psychological Investigation see*
  Gauld, A. O.
humanism 28
Hungary 146

Icheiser, G. 88, 164
idéologues 62, 107

ideology 4, 16, 23–6, 60, 103–5, 122–3; definition of 61
Ideology and Consciousness 149
institutions 124–5, 143

James, W. 33, 98
Járó, K. *see* Garai, L.
Jencks, C. 133, 165
joint action 81, 87
Jones, E. E. 74, 77, 165
Journal of Abnormal and Social Psychology 43, 165
Journal of Applied Psychology 30

Kamin, L. 38, 165
Karier, C. J. 38, 165
Kelley, H. H. 74, 76, 79, 85–6, 165
kettleness 132
Knowles, E. S. *see* Middlemist, R. D.
Köcski, M. *see* Garai, L.
Kuhn, T. 11–12, 24, 165

laboratory experiments 18–20, 31–2, 65
Lamal, P. A. 109, 165
Lamb, D. 109, 165
language 17, 24–6, 49, 52, 131–2
Latin America 154
Le Bon, G. 35–6, 62, 145, 165
Le Corbusier, C.-É. J. 133
Left, The 55, 86, 135, 140
Legris, J.-L. *see* Bryson, K.
Lenin, V. I. 40, 145
Lévi-Strauss, C. 55, 78, 103, 118, 122, 165
Liberman, K. 117–19, 165
literary theory 104, 120–3, 147
Lloyd, J. *see* Adams, D.
Lock, A. *see* Heelas, P.
Luckmann, T. *see* Berger, P.
Lyotard, J.-F. 46, 74, 165
Lysenko, T. 21

McDougall, W. 35, 36, 42, 152, 165
Machiavelli, N. die 27
McHugh, P. *see* Blum, A.
MacIntyre, A. 109, 137, 165

Marin, G. 154, 165
Marsh, P. 51, 142–3, 165
Matter, C. F. *see* Middlemist, R. D.
Mead, G. H. 16, 20, 33, 98, 165
metanarratives 2, 132, 137
Mexico City 154
middlemist 132
Middlemist, R. D. 18, 165
Milgram, S. 14, 26, 56, 166
Modern Age 62–3, 82–3; *see also* modernity
modernity 2, 46, 48, 63
Moscovici, S. 15–16, 24, 91–107, 109, 166
movements 22
mundane realism 54, 144

Nambikwara 122
Neitzsche, F. 115
new paradigm 11–12; *see also* new social psychology
new social psychology 4–5, 11–12, 20–3, 50–5, 101, 142–5
Nisbett, R. E. 77, 166
Norris, C. 159, 166

objects 44–5, 105
O'Donnell, J. M. 31–2, 166
Order of Things, The 62
ordinary explanation 72–89
ordinary language 25–6, 117

paradigms 11–12
Paris 1968 15, 55
Parker, I. 25, 46, 63, 97, 99, 102, 135, 150, 166
Pawley, M. 134, 166
perception 11, 154
Plague, The 64
Plon, M. 17, 146, 166
pluralism 137, 150
politics 59–60, 141–57
positivism 34
postmodernity 1–2, 46, 74, 131–40, 149, 151; definition of 133
post-philosophy 109
post-structuralism 1, 2, 55–6, 133

Potter, J. 101–2, 108, 110, 115, 137, 148, 160, 166
power 4, 26–7, 64–6, 122; definition of 65
powers 26–7
practical order 21, 27, 106
pragmatism 33
progress 11, 154
psychoanalysis 31, 91, 160
Psychologists' League 14

racism 14, 37–9, 43–4, 152
rationality 76–7
realism 54, 143; mundane realism 54, 144
reflexivity 133, 138
reification 93
reified universe 93
relativism 84–5, 140
representation 63, 102, 104–6
repression 30
resistance see power
rhetoric 80, 156
Right, The 139–40
Ring, K. 16, 166
Rorty, R. 109, 167
Rose, N. see Adlam, D.
Ross, E. A. 35
Rosser, E. see Marsh, P.
rules 52; for radicals 154–6
Russia 41, 138, 145

Salfield, A. see Adlam, D.
Sampson, E. E. 149, 167
Saussure, F. de 49–53, 57, 94, 138, 167
Schopler, J. 26, 167
Secord, P. F. 12, 22, 44, 52, 54, 158, 164
Seidel, G. 140, 167
self 27–8
self-presentation 82
semiology 49–53; see also Saussure, F. de
semiotic sociolinguistics see Liberman, K.
sexism 25, 155
shared meaning 101

Shaver, K. G. 76, 167
Shotter, J. 23, 25, 49, 54, 81, 86–8, 100, 113, 143–4, 150, 158, 167; see also Gauld, A. O.
signification 105–6
signifieds 50, 94
signifiers 50, 94
signs 49–50, 94
Silverman, D. 119–20, 167
Skinner, B. F. 109
Smith, S. 145, 167
Smoke, K. 37, 167
social cognition 88–9, 98–100
Social Cognition: Perspectives on Everyday Understanding see Forgas, J.
social facilitation 13, 20, 29
social representations 88–107
Society for the Psychological Study of Social Issues 14
sociology 32, 95–8
South Africa 152
Soviet Union 21, 145–6; Soviet social psychology 145–6
Spain 14
Spearman, C. 37
speech 58–9, 86
Spencer, H. 37
Stanley, L. 26, 153, 167
structuralism 49, 55
Squire, C. 153, 167
subjects 29, 44–5, 53, 65, 139, 149

Taylor, F. W. 39, 40, 145, 167
Taylorism see Taylor, F. W.
Taylor, S. E. see Fiske, S. T.
templates 54
Terman, L. 31, 37
text 56–9, 110, 120–5; definition of 57
textual sociology 115–21
The 2nd January Group 137, 167
Titchener, E. B. 31–2, 34, 42, 167
Torode, B. see Silverman, D.
Totman, R. 75–6, 81, 84–5, 88, 167
Triplett, N. 13, 29, 41, 168
truth 45–6, 107

Ustinov, P. 138, 168

Venn, C. *see* Adlam, D.,
  Henriques, J.
Veres, S. *see* Garai, L.
Vico, G. 144
Völkerpsychologie see Wundt,
  W.
Völkseele see Wundt, W.

Walkerdine, V. *see* Adlam, D.,
  Henriques, J.

Watson, J. B. 132
Weber, M. 95–9, 168
Weber, S. 124, 168
Wetherell, M. *see* Potter, J.
Wilkinson, S. 153, 168
Williamson, J. 132, 168
Wise S. *see* Stanley, L.
Wittgenstein, L. 109
writing 58–9
Wundt, W. 34, 41–2, 98

Young, R. 139, 147, 168